GREEN LIVING

Brimming with creative inspiration, how-to projects, and useful information to enrich your everyday life, quarto.com is a favorite destination for those pursuing their interests and passions.

© 2022 Quarto Publishing Group USA Inc.

First published in 2022 by Rock Point,
an imprint of The Quarto Group,
142 West 36th Street, 4th Floor,
New York, NY 10018 USA
T (212) 779-4972 F (212) 779-6058
www.Quarto.com

Rock Point titles are also available at discount for retail, wholesale, promotional, and bulk purchase. For details, contact the Special Sales Manager by email at specialsales@quarto.com or by mail at The Quarto Group, Attn: Special Sales Manager, 100 Cummings Center Suite 265D, Beverly, MA 01915, USA.

Library of Congress Cataloging-in-Publication Data

Names: Green Matters (Organization), author.
Title: Green living : a comprehensive guide to a happy and sustainable life
  / Green Matters.
Description: New York : Rock Point, 2022. | Includes bibliographical
  references and index. | Summary: "Who says living a green lifestyle has
  to be a chore? Part reference, part lifestyle-with a dash of
  inspiration-Green Living is full of approachable, accessible, and easily
  implemented strategies to quickly and easily bring sustainability into
  all areas of your life and home"-- Provided by publisher.
Identifiers: LCCN 2021038796 (print) | LCCN 2021038797 (ebook) | ISBN
  9781631067204 (hardcover) | ISBN 9780760368398 (ebook)
Subjects: LCSH: Sustainable living--Handbooks, manuals, etc. | Home
  economics--Handbooks, manuals, etc.
Classification: LCC GE196 .G746 2022 (print) | LCC GE196 (ebook) | DDC
  640.28/6--dc23
LC record available at https://lccn.loc.gov/2021038796
LC ebook record available at https://lccn.loc.gov/2021038797

10 9 8 7 6 5 4 3 2 1

ISBN: 978-1-63106-720-4

Publisher: Rage Kindelsperger
Creative Director: Laura Drew
Managing Editor: Cara Donaldson
Interior Design: Ashley Prine
Cover Design: Laura Drew

Printed in China

Printed on 100% post-consumer waste recycled paper using vegetable-based inks.

GREEN
LIVING

A Comprehensive Guide to a Happy and Sustainable Life

GREENMATTERS

ROCK
POINT
QUARTOKNOWS.COM
NEW YORK, NY

Contents

Introduction

Headlines about the numerous ecological crises the world is suffering are all too common nowadays. They can seem alarmist and are frequently dismissed as such by governments and corporations that are resistant to change. Even the media outlets that write these stories are sometimes accused of propagandizing by their competitors. Given the climate of fear in the world and the overwhelming nature of the problems that spark such headlines, our instinct is to turn away from the clamor and only tend to our own lives. But the truth is that by making manageable changes to our everyday lives, we can have a big impact on the direction the world is heading.

The truth is that disaster headlines are part of our own lives. Even though we may not live in an area ravaged by fires or air made toxic by water pollution, we can see the evidence of environmental breakdown on our own shores. Hurricanes and tornadoes are becoming more frequent and much more powerful; our national forests are falling to wildfires and disease problems; the Midwest is experiencing increasingly devastating flooding while California has been in a severe drought for over a decade.

The planet is getting smaller, not bigger, in a sense. The consequences of unbridled production and consumption are no longer "someone else's problem." Coal-fired production plants pollute the air worldwide. Single-use plastic cups, bottles, and straws of tourists from around the globe are trashing the beaches and reefs of the islands they go to see. Emissions from industrialized nations are causing acid rain and water pollution for themselves, their neighbors, and countries half a world away.

Don't Lose Hope!

The news is grim indeed, but while the biggest changes will have to come from the governments of the world, it is possible for each of us to make changes in our own lives that can have a meaningful impact on these formidable problems. We can each make meaningful change, but no single person can solve the climate crisis. We're going to need to work with corporations and oil companies to solve this disaster. And while some people share more of the blame than others for our current predicament, it is only through solidarity that we'll be able to solve this problem.

Our website, Green Matters, is for people looking to live more sustainably, fight the climate crisis, and learn about environmental justice. Our coverage brings awareness to issues surrounding the climate

crisis—as well as solutions. Our mission in this book is to make being green easy and accessible for all. We want to show you what to change in your own life that can make a real difference. The changes we as individuals can make are cumulative small acts that have profound impacts when enough people do them.

In each chapter, we'll detail different environmental issues and what you can do to help manage them. At the end of each chapter, we'll sum up the small, medium, and large steps you can take to help adjust your lifestyle to one that is "greener," that is, better for the environment and for sustaining life on Earth. (You'll find more in-depth explanations of how each step is categorized on the following page.) We hope to inspire you to make simple changes to your daily habits and lifestyle, and also to empower you to fight for what you believe in. We believe that many small actions can collectively make a big difference in ensuring a healthy planet for generations to come.

Any change you make to live a greener life helps make the world a cleaner, healthier, and more beautiful place for all of its inhabitants. The best thing we can all do is learn, try, and never give up hope.

✳ ✳ ✳

Actions You Can Take

SEED

Seed steps are the easiest changes to make and include things like reusing cardboard boxes for shipping and storage, or repurposing food jars as organizers for office or craft supplies.

SPROUT

Sprout steps require a little more effort in changing the way we think about living our lives. Examples of Sprout steps include being strict about recycling everything you can, or switching to an electric rather than gas-powered vehicle.

TREE

Tree steps involve major lifestyle changes, such as buying only sustainably made versions of clothing and furniture, or converting your home's power system to solar or wind.

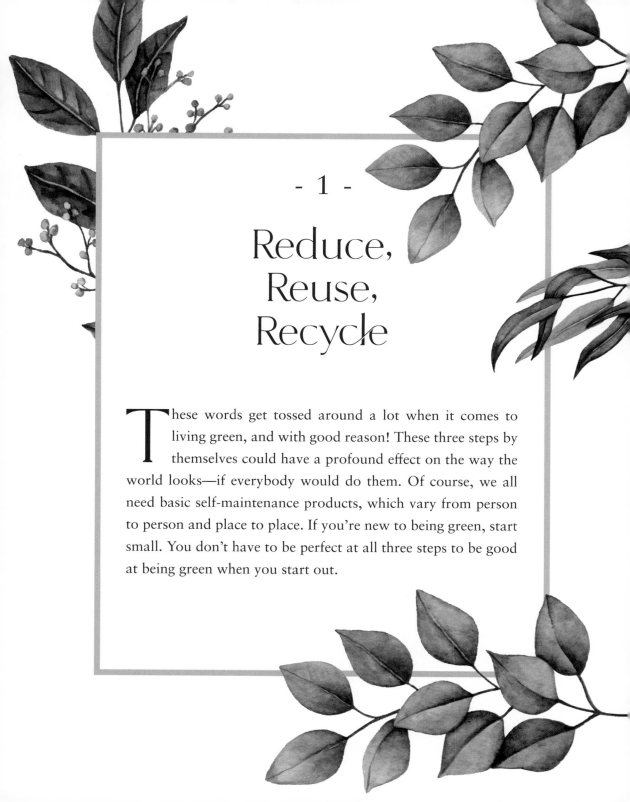

- 1 -

Reduce,
Reuse,
Recycle

These words get tossed around a lot when it comes to living green, and with good reason! These three steps by themselves could have a profound effect on the way the world looks—if everybody would do them. Of course, we all need basic self-maintenance products, which vary from person to person and place to place. If you're new to being green, start small. You don't have to be perfect at all three steps to be good at being green when you start out.

Reduce

Have you ever bought so much stuff that you were forced to buy boxes, bins, and bags to store the stuff in—then had to buy shelves to stack the boxes and bins on? Though saving items for times of scarcity can be helpful, we often simply do not need to have backup provisions for our backups. This scarcity mind-set is an example of consumerism gone wild, and our economy is one that especially encourages overconsumption. Nobody will ever forget the mad rush for toilet paper during the pandemic, as if it would never be produced again! The best way to reduce the amount that goes into the landfill is to decrease the demand for it.

Minimalism is a very green mind-set, but the possession-free life of a Zen master is a tall order for most of us. Rather, if you change your mind-set around consumption, you can help make the world a more sustainable place by not participating in the drive to use up all our resources. For instance, buying clothes every week can actually result in diminishing returns of happiness. Instead, if you employ famed organizing consultant Marie Kondo's catchphrase "Does it spark joy?" when looking at all the things you have accumulated, you can figure out what you really do and don't need. Getting rid of the surplus that doesn't serve you anymore, as you'll soon see, has a great number of benefits. Take note of when you have more than you need and could ever use by using the following Home Inventory.

The checklist shows some of the many household items a lot of us have that could be greatly reduced in number without changing our lives much. By paring down what you own, you'll save space, time spent taking care of all of these things, and the money you would spend to keep replacing them. By taking stock of what you have and comparing it to what you actually use, you can reduce what you buy in the future. You can be conscientious about whether you really need to buy more clothes, more office supplies, more electronics, more cereal you never finish before it goes stale, or if you already have what you need.

The checklist also shows you the things you're not actually using and can be rehomed to a place where they will be more appreciated. You can think of this as doing more for your community, because by rehoming what you own but don't use, you often make things available that might otherwise be financially prohibitive and inaccessible for people who really want them. Rehoming also means that whoever is getting your old stuff doesn't have to buy new products that consume more resources in manufacturing and packaging. It's a double win! Be conscious about where you rehome your things by trying to make sure unwanted items are going to people and institutions that will use them. The goal is to try and keep trash out of landfills.

HOME INVENTORY

What in your house don't you use? This list will help you determine what items can be rehomed.

Media & Entertainment

- Books
- Magazines
- Movies
- Toys and games

Electronics

- TVs
- Computers
- Video game consoles
- Phones
- Tablets
- Cameras
- Printers

Office Supplies

- Paper
- Pens
- Scissors
- Tape dispensers
- Staplers

Clothing & Bedding

- Clothes
- Shoes
- Accessories
- Blankets
- Sheets
- Towels
- Linens

Pantry

- Cereals
- Beverages
- Snack foods
- Condiments

Tools

- Home repair
- Gardening
- Automotive
- Crafting supplies

Appliances

- Odd appliances
- Hot dog warmer
- Bread maker
- Waffle iron
- Indoor grill
- Omelet maker

Personal Care

- Hair dryer
- Curling iron
- Cosmetics
- Skin care

Rehoming Within Your Community

There are lots of resources online for rehoming your surplus items. A Facebook group called Buy Nothing is localized to the area in which you live or work; people can post items they want to give away or are in need of. The listings are free of charge. This system of giving away or trading goods and services is called "bartering" or sometimes a waste-moving or "gift" economy.

Buy Nothing groups are just one place where you instantly have access to hundreds or even thousands of people in your community, one of whom would be glad to take that unused bag of golf clubs or the 30 pounds of tomatoes you harvested from your garden this year. Search your community for individuals and groups willing to barter for goods and services. Colleges, community service centers, clubs, churches, and care centers often put up notices for swap meets and other gatherings where items can be exchanged.

In addition to material goods, you can find and offer services such as haircuts, yoga sessions, yard care, or music lessons. Barter groups can help grow community ties. The person who swooned over your grandma's old set of dishes might wind up becoming your new neighborhood pal.

Freecycle is one group that has existed on its own website for nearly 20 years. A good place to start looking for a group is Google, using search terms like "buy nothing" or "swap and trade." Facebook has its "Find a

GO YOUR OWN WAY

If there isn't a system or cause that you feel comfortable with, or if you have items that don't fit any specific causes, there's another way you can get rid of things that no longer "spark joy" while still supporting a cause you believe in. You can sell your clothing—either in a yard/garage sale or on a reselling app or website, such as Poshmark, eBay, or ThredUP—and donate the funds to a cause you support. That way, you are extending the life of your garments, which is essential for sustainability and waste reduction.

group" page where you can find Buy Nothing or similar groups. The Buy Nothing group page has an index to other Buy Nothing groups across the nation. When posting, the key is that the items must be free, not for sale.

Schools and religious organizations are probably the best candidates for clothing drives (especially coat drives when the weather turns cold), but in most cities you can find shelters and organizations that will take your donations directly and give them to the people they serve.

Another option is donating your un-wanted items to a shop affiliated with a local charity. That way you know the money raised from the items sold will directly benefit a specific, local cause and it's unlikely that your clothes (or the money raised) will leave your community.

Reuse and Repurpose

The key to reusing and repurposing is to think outside the box—literally. If you can think of yourself as a closed system, one where you repurpose old things for different reasons, you can slowly but surely reduce the amount of waste you make and items you buy by reusing things that would otherwise just go into a landfill.

Repurposing Textiles

For example, think about old blankets, sheets, or towels that you would throw away. Most animal shelters are always in need of these items to use as bedding for their animals; best practice would be to call before taking the items to the shelter. Additionally, old towels can be cut up and used as rags for cleaning around the house rather than buying new towels or throwaway cleaning wipes. Bed pillows that have lost their fluffiness can become chair or bench cushions; if they are filled with batting or loose fiber (*not* rubber foam), the stuffing can be pulled out and set out in string bags for birds and squirrels to use as nesting material.

Reusing Boxes

Instead of buying storage containers, you can reuse bottles, jars, and boxes to store everything from sugar, flour, and pasta to cotton balls, nails, and underwear. Cardboard boxes can be cut to any size and shape, and then decorated with paint, wallpaper, or fabric, if desired. Most store-bought storage boxes are just cardboard anyway. No sewing skills are required to cut fabric to fit a box

DEFINE YOUR TERMS

Reusing: When we reuse something, we do not change its original state or purpose. Washing out a glass bottle and refilling it for another purpose is reusing it, not recycling it (see the definition of recycling on page 16). Many people reuse gift paper to wrap another present, or use frayed kitchen towels to clean the car. The difference between repurposing and reusing is not critical.

and attach it with hot glue. Boxes can be custom-sized and decorated to fit any color scheme or décor style.

Secondhand Is Grand

Reuse isn't just about what you have, it's also about things you may need. Instead of buying new, consider reusing items from others. Thrift stores are a treasure trove of reusables. Decorative glass and baskets are plentiful and cheap there. Furniture is a particular bargain at thrift and consignment stores, and is therefore sometimes hard to come by. Sports equipment, cookware and bakeware, dishes, and glasses can be found by the dozens. Clothing is abundant and in good condition; you might even score barely worn designer goods, especially in upscale areas.

Repurposing and Reusing Clothing

Worn or outgrown clothing doesn't have to remain clothing. A shrunken sweater can become a scarf or hat with some basic sewing skills. In the absence of such skills, the sweater can still be a cozy bed for a cat or small dog.

The United States is the largest exporter of secondhand clothes, but it's important to make sure you know where your clothes are going to end up when you donate them. Do some research before donating. The best choices involve the clothing being donated directly to those in

DEFINE YOUR TERMS

Repurposing: To repurpose something is to change its original purpose but not its original state—for example, using newspaper as gift wrap. It's still a newspaper, but you're not using it as such. Or you can wash out used baby-food jars and use them to store thumbtacks and paper clips. This may sound like reusing rather than repurposing because you are not changing the jar's purpose (storage), but it's no longer a food container. The line between reusing and repurposing is indeed fuzzy, and you can read the definition of reusing on page 13.

IN GOOD COMPANY

Here are some national organizations that will distribute clothing and other donations directly to those who need them.

TerraCycle specializes in repurposing and recycling unusual items. Its Fabrics and Clothing Zero Waste Box lets you buy a box from the company, fill it with clothing and fabric (no matter what condition it's in), and ship it to TerraCycle for repurposing.

Soles4Souls is a national shoe-recycling program.

Dress for Success operates in more than 150 cities in 30 countries, and that list is constantly growing. The New York City–based nonprofit aims to improve the lives of women by helping them find jobs and secure financial independence, among other things. Dress for Success gives clothes directly to women in need, so it collects mostly women's professional wear. Its general rule to consider when donating is "Would you feel comfortable wearing this on an interview?" According to its 2017 annual report, Dress for Success celebrated its 20th anniversary by helping to dress more than 74,000 women.

Room to Grow understands that babies and children are constantly growing and seem to outgrow their clothes overnight. This creates two problems: The first is that parents constantly have clothes that they no longer need or can use; the second is that some parents who can't necessarily afford a lot for their child are constantly struggling because their purchases don't last long. Enter Room to Grow. This company accepts baby and toddler clothing, as well as toys, books, play mats, bibs, bassinets, potties, high chairs, and so on, which are donated to families in need. Room to Grow, which has chapters in New York City and Boston, works with parents for the first three years of a child's life, providing not only clothing and necessary products related to child-rearing, but also support from a licensed social worker during those critical years.

need, rather than it being sold for a profit and then donated afterward. While some organizations operate retail stores with the intention of raising money for important causes, many times these operations sell their clothes in bulk internationally, creating a supply that is significantly larger than the demand. Typically, these extras end up in landfills.

If you are fortunate enough to have too much clothing, there are a number of companies besides thrift stores (which frequently have more clothes than they really want) that are happy to repurpose these items for you. The best thing to do is donate or sell your goods in a way that goes direct to consumers, rather than something like a thrift store that may sell them overseas. In the best-case scenario, if you give clothing to an organization for business clothes, they will give it to someone who needs a job.

Recycle

Recycling is vital in helping stop the amount of trash going to already-overflowing landfills. No one wants a new garbage dump near their home, but the landfills in use can't take the staggering amount of trash we throw away every day in this country. When landfills exceed their capacity, they create a number of serious environmental problems, from toxic chemical leakage to air and water pollution. Recycling is fairly simple; all that's required is a place to sort the materials. A surprising number of things are recyclable beyond the common glass, paper, and plastic.

Aluminum

Aluminum is the best-known recyclable material. Aluminum cans are 100 percent recyclable, and can be made into new cans

DEFINE YOUR TERMS

Recycling: Broadly, *recycling* means turning something that was previously used for one purpose into something else. In practice, recycling involves using chemical or mechanical methods to break down simple materials like glass, paper, and certain plastics into their most basic state so that this material can be reused to make a completely new product. For example, glass bottles might be melted down or crushed and turned into glass tiles, or used computer paper might be pulped to make stationery or greeting cards. It's this changing of the material from its original state to a different form that defines recycling.

over and over again. In fact, it's estimated that 75 percent of the total aluminum ever produced is still being used today. It actually takes 95 percent *less* energy to recycle old aluminum cans into new ones than it does to make new ones from scratch. Each can that is recycled saves enough energy to light a room in a house for 3 hours or power an iPod for 20! An aluminum can will be recycled and back on the shelf within 60 days.

In an average year, Americans save the energy equivalent of 825 million gallons of crude oil (enough to fill 10 supertankers) by recycling aluminum. Shockingly, however, every three months we still *throw away* enough potentially recyclable aluminum to rebuild and replace every commercial airplane in US fleets. Finland, Germany, and Brazil are the aluminum recycling champs, each recovering and recycling over 98 percent of the aluminum they use each year.

Glass

Glass is another material that is endlessly recyclable and never loses its quality or purity. In the United States, we recycle only about 26 percent of our overall glass, and over 40 percent of *that* is just beer and drink bottles. Glass is simple to recycle; it usually doesn't need to be sorted by color and labels don't have to be removed. Glass containers should be rinsed clean of food particles, but they don't have to be

BIG NUMBERS A study from MIT showed that 60 percent of the more than 1 BILLION pounds of trash thrown away by Americans on a daily basis is actually recyclable.

thoroughly washed. Recycle the lids with metals, not with the glass.

In addition to being repurposed for storage, glass bottles can be used for decorative objects, craft projects, and even garden borders.

Paper

We could make a huge dent in the amount of trash going to landfills if we would just recycle our paper. Most of the paper being recycled in the United States currently comes from commercial business programs. We need to step up as individuals and do our part. Recycle *all* your paper and campaign for it in the establishments that you frequent. But remember, for paper to be recycled it must be free of grease and food bits; used pizza boxes and fast-food containers are not candidates for recycling. Neither are boxes that have waxy coatings or have been covered with plastic or other decorative materials.

BIG NUMBERS Across the globe, more than 4 billion trees are cut down each year to make paper. That's the equivalent of 1.7 billion acres of Amazon rain forest *every year*. Every American uses about 700 pounds of paper products a year, about half of which gets recycled. Paper is highly recyclable, yet 40 percent of all municipal waste is paper—over 70 million tons' worth.

Plastic

If there's a problem child of recycling, it's plastic. While some plastics are completely recyclable, others are not. We need to make an effort to recycle every piece of plastic we use. Germany, Wales, and Singapore are the top countries in the world for recycling, with each recycling over 60 percent of their total waste. The United States lags far behind at just under

PICK THE RIGHT PACKAGING!

Where it's not possible to buy foods and other products from bulk bins using your own reusable containers, choose those packaged in cans, glass bottles and jars, or paper/cardboard wrappings. Metals in particular are highly recyclable—especially steel and aluminum. Buying products in cans is much more environmentally sound than buying anything in plastic. Glass and paper, while they have lower rates of recycling, are still better than plastic. If you are buying something in plastic, check its code first to see if you'll be able to recycle it.

PAPER RECYCLING AND REUSE

Here are some great tips on what you can do with your used paper products:

Recyclable Paper Products

- Notebook, computer paper, stationery

- Mail, envelopes, catalogs (staples OK)

- Wrapping paper, gift bags

- Toilet paper and paper towel rolls (not the paper itself)

- Phone books, computer manuals

- Paperback books, magazines, newspapers

- Paper bags

- Cereal and prepared-food boxes

- Cardboard shipping boxes

- Cardboard egg cartons

Paper You Can't Recycle

- Used pizza boxes

- Fast-food containers

- Wax-coated boxes

- Boxes covered with plastic or other decorative elements

Reuses for Newspaper

- Liners for bird and small mammal cages (make sure the paper is printed with soy ink, just to be safe).

- Crumpled up, it leaves a streak-free, lint-free shine when used to clean glass. You can still recycle the paper after that!

- Excellent packing material for shipping.

- Bound stacks make good insulation for interior home walls if your local building codes allow it. (Free newspapers are available from many recycling centers, which are happy to get rid of excess.)

30 percent of total waste, and less than 25 percent of recyclable plastic.

PET (which stands for polyethylene terephthalate and is a kind of polyester) is the most widely recycled plastic in the world; approximately 1.5 billion pounds of it are recycled in the United States each year. Recycling the material uses 60 percent less energy than that required to make new plastic. This, in turn, lowers greenhouse gas emissions to the atmosphere and greatly reduces the amount of trash going to landfills. Like aluminum, PET is endlessly recyclable and can be made into all sorts of new products, such as car parts, carpet, clothing (especially shoes), industrial packaging, and more.

Since plastics are resistant to decomposition, they take up an enormous amount of space in landfills. Consider how much space an empty gallon jug occupies. If all plastic bottles were flattened prior to being thrown away, a lot of space would be saved, but they would still remain in the landfill

for 100 years or more. Additionally, most plastic containers are specifically designed to *resist* flattening.

One such way to reduce the amount of plastic we use is to pursue the new possibility in plastic packaging: vegetable starches. Cornstarch and cellulose (which makes up plant cell walls), and root vegetables like potato, cassava, and taro, are currently being explored as sources for completely biodegradable plastics. Though in limited use right now, these plastic alternatives encourage more experimentation and production of such materials.

Plastics other than PET can be recycled, though it varies which ones are accepted by local recycling centers. Even if your center doesn't accept non-PET plastic, a business near you might. A quick online search will likely turn up places you can bring these items.

Most plastic containers and other items made from recyclable plastic display a code in the form of a number inside an arrow that identifies the plastic material.

BIG NUMBERS It's estimated that each US household throws away about 36 pounds of completely reusable PET every year. There are an estimated 130 million households in the United States, meaning that we are wasting 4.68 billion pounds of PET each year. That's nearly five times the amount we are actually recycling.

Steel

Steel is the most successfully recycled material in North America, with a recycle rate of nearly 90 percent. That's higher than the rates of glass, paper, plastic, and aluminum combined. Steel comes from cars, bicycles, appliances, construction refuse, and steel cans. Depending on your area, you may need to bring steel items to your

PLASTIC RECYCLING CODES

Here is a quick list of recycling codes with some examples
of the products you'll usually see them used on:

Code 1: PET

(aka PETE) is a chemical derived from the by-products of petroleum refining (as are most plastics). It is identified by recycling Code 1. In addition to beverages, PET containers can hold frozen foods, condiments, and liquid medications such as cough syrup and antacids.

Code 2: HDPE

(high-density polyethylene) is used for sturdier plastic bottles, such as those for laundry detergents, motor oil, bleach, soaps and gels, and milk.

Code 3: PVC

(polyvinyl chloride) is found in many kinds of plastic tubing, including that for plumbing, medical equipment, and coating electrical wires. It's also used for packing materials, shampoo bottles, and spray bottles.

Code 4: LDPE

(low-density polyethylene) is used to make soft squeezable bottles and toys, as well as most plastic bags (dry cleaning, grocery and retail bags, bread and sandwich bags, etc.). While this material is recyclable, not many recycling centers will accept it. Many grocery and some retail stores, however, will take plastic bags back for recycling—or you can always reuse the bag for shopping.

Code 5: PP

(polypropylene) is resistant to heat and is used to contain liquids that are heat-processed, such as ketchup and syrup. It is also used for products such as straws, bottle caps, furniture, luggage, some toys, and car parts from bumpers to door panels.

Code 6: PS

(polystyrene) is a versatile material commonly used to make Styrofoam and other soft foam products for packing materials, egg cartons, and disposable dishware. It is occasionally still found in fast-food containers, though most fast-food companies have gone to some type of paper packaging for their products. Polystyrene can also be used to make hard plastics for toys, CD cases, and appliance trays.

Code 7: This is an

oddball category for most plastics that don't fit into any of the first six groups, including acrylics, nylon, and fiberglass. Be aware that Code 7 items are commonly not accepted at local recycling centers due to the special equipment required to break them down. In this category are things like five-gallon plastic water jugs (so many uses for these!), oven baking bags, baby bottles and sippy cups, and car parts.

local recycling center or arrange to have them picked up through the public works department.

Steel wire is highly recyclable, but requires special equipment to shred it without tangling in the machinery. For this reason, most local recycling centers won't accept wire (usually in the form of wire clothes hangers).

Biowaste

Biowaste is a broad term for recyclable material that comes from biological remains (mainly plant). Construction lumber, yard trimmings, leaves, tree branches, cornstalks, and weeds are all examples of biowaste. Less obvious examples are animal manure and used vegetable oil from restaurant fryers.

Most of this material is compostable, but some of it can be used in less common ways. Used vegetable oil can be utilized as vehicle fuel, with some modifications to the engine. Animal manure is an especially fine fertilizer, but should be "aged" for several months to allow the uric acid in the waste to break down before it is applied to the garden. Otherwise, the acid will burn the plant roots and kill the plants. Never use manure from dogs or cats: It doesn't have enough nitrogen to be beneficial to plants, and the smell will draw other dogs and cats to your garden. Use the dirty water from your fresh (not salt) water fish tank on your houseplants and watch them grow like crazy!

Electronics

Recycling electronics is big business. Electronic and electrical machinery is termed "e-waste." In addition to refurbishing older electronics such as phones and computers for reuse, there are thousands of components in defective and obsolete electrical devices that can be stripped out and recycled. There are legitimate concerns, however, about the health impacts of potential exposure to toxic materials in modern electronics. If you wish to recycle your own tech, call your area's electronics stores to find out which ones participate in a recycling program.

In addition to the precious metals in electronics, however, there are toxic metals such as cadmium, lead, and mercury that present poisoning hazards to workers who handle them. This is the concern with the unregulated recycling of these materials

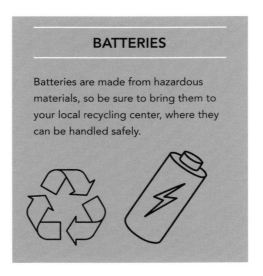

BATTERIES

Batteries are made from hazardous materials, so be sure to bring them to your local recycling center, where they can be handled safely.

BIG NUMBERS Less than 20 percent of all e-waste is recycled properly. Either the rest winds up in landfills, where it can leak toxic metals into the soil and water, or a smaller portion is sent to certain developing countries where hand labor is cheap. Gold, palladium, silver, copper, and tin are valuable metals that can be recovered from circuit boards and wiring. In fact, it's estimated that over 5 percent of all the gold in the world is currently tied up in e-waste. There is 100 times more gold per ton of e-waste than there is per ton of gold ore!

The Consumer Electronics Association estimates that the useful life of a cell phone is less than five years; this means that somewhere around 200 million cell phones are replaced in the United States every five years. The 15,000 pounds of gold recoverable from this many phones is the equivalent of about 600 standard-size solid gold bars—enough to cover an area 10 feet by 10 feet, 2 inches deep. And that's just the gold!

The Environmental Protection Agency (EPA) estimates that recycling just 1 million mobile phones per year in the United States will recover more than 750 pounds of silver, 75 pounds of gold, 30 pounds of palladium, and 35,000 pounds of copper.

in developing countries. Many of these operations use hand labor to dismantle the components, and then use highly corrosive acids, such as sulfuric, hydrochloric, or nitric acid, to leach the precious metals from the pieces. This leaching releases the toxic metals as well, and the runoff contaminates groundwater.

The safest recycling centers use huge machines to shred nonreusable electronics into quarter-size pieces, which are then further processed mechanically to separate the valuable metals while the remaining waste is eventually sent to incinerators. These furnaces are equipped with scrubbers to prevent toxic metals in the waste from being emitted into the air.

The best thing you can do is rehome electronics that are still working using the methods we talked about earlier in this chapter (see pages 10). For nonworking electronics, you may be able to bring them to your local recycling center. Electronics stores also often take in old phones, computers, and other devices for recycling. No matter what you do with an old device, make sure you delete all personal data, passwords, and accounts from it before getting rid of it.

✳ ✳ ✳

Actions You Can Take

SEED

Recycle everything you can. Use your curbside recycling program if one is offered and commit to not throwing away recyclable materials! Sorting and cleaning them is quick and easy. Consciously recycle all of the packaging while taking note of the garbage you inadvertently accept into your home when you shop for things you need.

SPROUT

Reuse and repurpose. Get creative before you throw anything away. Can you think of another use for it? If not, can you sell or donate it instead of throwing it away?

TREE

Buy only necessities. Think about how your items are packaged and the waste they can come with, and take steps to make sure that you aren't creating more waste where you don't have to. While the best thing you can do is reduce, if you already have something, reuse or recycle it. Think of the things you purchase and the things that are already in your home as part of a cycle. Buy only necessities in material goods and try not to buy anything new. Avoid buying duplicate electronics and tech or specialty appliances unless they're something you'll use frequently (twice a month or more). Find package-free stores to buy these goods. If you're able, employ local craftspeople and businesses to source and create complex things that you can't readily make yourself.

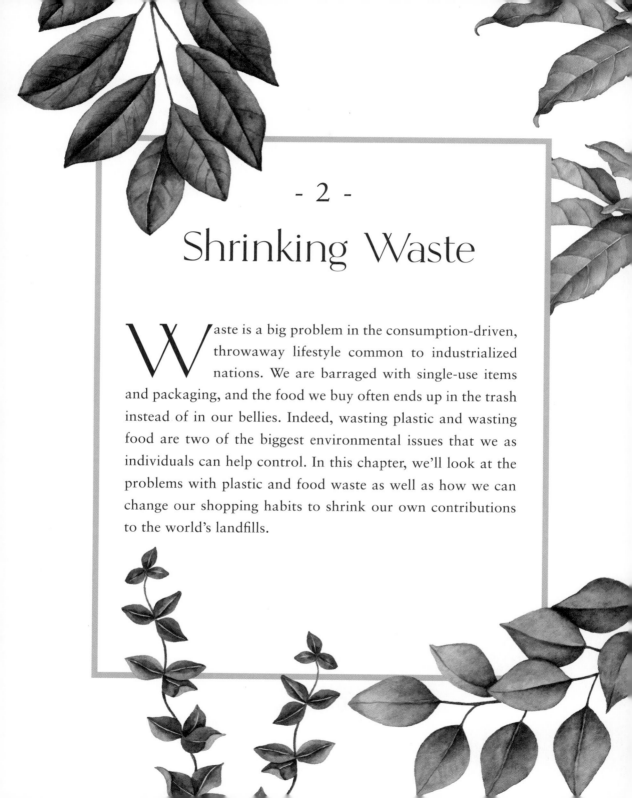

- 2 -

Shrinking Waste

Waste is a big problem in the consumption-driven, throwaway lifestyle common to industrialized nations. We are barraged with single-use items and packaging, and the food we buy often ends up in the trash instead of in our bellies. Indeed, wasting plastic and wasting food are two of the biggest environmental issues that we as individuals can help control. In this chapter, we'll look at the problems with plastic and food waste as well as how we can change our shopping habits to shrink our own contributions to the world's landfills.

Plastic Problems

The world is currently designed around plastic use, and as consumers, we often don't have much control over how products are presented to us. But there are many ways we can decrease our own use of plastics and subsequently impact manufacturing methods. The things we buy—and refuse to buy—is how we shape the world through our spending. First, let's look at what all this plastic is doing to the planet.

Currently, 500 *billion* single-use plastic bags are thrown away every year—enough to encircle the Earth 4,200 times in a meter-wide strip. Ocean Crusaders, a charity focused on waterway cleaning, estimates that more than 100,000 marine animals and a million birds die each year due to becoming entangled in plastic trash. An estimated two-thirds of all fish are believed to be suffering from plastic ingestion.

Single-use plastic waste (whether as a straw in its entirety or as broken up bits of microplastic) is rife with potential hazards to sea creatures, which consume these nonbiodegradable plastics. Cutting the straws into small pieces before throwing them away doesn't help, because the pieces float in water and are even easier for marine life to ingest.

An equally serious though less obvious problem is the rise of microplastic particles in our waters. As plastics degrade, they shed particles known as microplastics. These particles may be so small they can't be seen with the naked eye; however, the small particles are subjected to a greater amount of environmental abrasion than large plastic items, and they are even more prone to releasing chemical toxins into the environment. Ocean Crusaders estimates that over 1.5 billion plastic microparticles per square mile currently pollute the ocean floors.

According to studies done on behalf of the United Nations, there is not a single square mile of ocean surface that is not contaminated by plastic pollution. Ocean currents known as "gyres" come together

DEFINE YOUR TERMS

Biodegradable: This is a term for something that can be broken down by microorganisms in the environment. "Biodegradable" is sometimes confused with "recyclable," but they aren't the same. Recyclable materials can be reused to make other things, but refashioning them into new products requires energy resources and mechanical intervention. Some materials, such as wood and natural fibers like cotton and linen, are *both* biodegradable and recyclable.

in certain spots across the globe, and in these places the plastic waste forms giant floating garbage islands. The largest of these, known as the Great Pacific Garbage Patch, currently covers an area the size of Texas, New Mexico, Oklahoma, Louisiana, and Missouri *combined*.

There *is* hope! While the world is literally swimming in plastic, change is possible. For example, beginning in 2010, Great Britain instituted a 5-pence tax (equivalent to about $0.06 US) on each plastic bag used. Within five years, plastic bag use in Great Britain was reduced by a whopping 80 percent! Now, that's a government-imposed tax, but it shows how much change can be achieved by a small adjustment in how people shop.

Ditch Single-Use Plastics

While plastics manufacturing probably isn't going away any time soon, we can help reduce the amount of plastic waste that enters our landfills and waterways.

One way is to decrease the amount of bottled water we buy. Of all the wasteful habits people have, not buying bottled water will have the greatest impact on trash reduction and decreasing plastic pollution in the ocean.

By getting a glass, metal, or even a multiuse plastic water bottle and refilling it throughout the day, you'll save hundreds of dollars a year, eliminate tons of landfill waste, and decrease the demand for plastic. Likewise, choose reusable food and beverage containers whenever possible. For example, you can bring your own containers to restaurants to take home your leftovers.

Carrying reusable shopping bags is another easy and effective change you can make. Eco-friendly totes can be rolled up and kept in your bag or car so that whenever you go shopping, you can use your own bags instead of the store's single-use plastic ones.

Eliminating our addiction to plastic straws is an important consideration. For people with certain physical limitations, straws are critical to their ability to eat and drink safely. Some of those people can substitute reusable stainless-steel straws, but for others, that's not an option. The "straw bans" that are rising up in some communities are discriminatory to some people. Those of us who are using straws simply out of habit or preference, however, are the ones who should be looking for alternatives to our plastic straw habits.

PLASTICS TO PASS ON

Plastic is practically everywhere. Here are some products you might not even realize have plastic in them but are better off avoided when possible:

Chip and Snack Bags

They may not seem like plastic, but unless they're paper-based, they're probably petroleum-based.

Feminine Products

Applicators and even pads and tampons themselves often are made of synthetic materials that contain plastic. Cotton alternatives are becoming more available.

Individually Wrapped

This means lots and lots of plastic is being used in the packaging.

Takeout Containers

These often aren't recyclable, and they have the added disadvantage of usually coming bundled in single-use plastic bags. See if your favorite spots will let you bring your own containers or at least your own bags.

Microbeads

Those little exfoliating beads in body washes and scrubs are often made of plastic. They even show up in some whitening toothpastes.

Sponges

Most cleaning sponges contain plastic, so you might want to consider switching to washable rags or look for products that boast being plastic-free.

When you do find yourself having to buy something that comes in plastic, check the code and do your best to only buy products that come in recyclable plastic containers, which may mean saying goodbye to a favorite brand.

Reuse or Repurpose Packaging

When you find yourself with some packaging, you can often repurpose it. While ways to reuse bottles and cans are obvious, there are many ways to reuse packaging that you might not have thought of:

- Save used plastic bags from frozen foods or bread wrappers to pick up your dog's poop while out walking. You can also scoop used cat litter into these bags and dispose of it. The plastic bags aren't recyclable, so getting double use out of them is thinking green.
- Plastic containers with lids can have all sorts of new uses: for carrying leftovers from restaurants (wash and reuse again

and again) and for storing everything from paper clips to safety pins, nuts and candy, to nuts and bolts.

- Large cardboard boxes can be a dream come true for kids to play with—let them go crazy! You can help them turn appliance boxes into castles and furniture boxes into rockets. Used cardboard boxes can also hold kids' toys, office records, or winter clothes. Cardboard is much better for storing clothing than those plastic bins you buy, because it lets fabrics breathe, which helps prevent mildew.

BIG NUMBERS Across the globe, more than 1 million plastic bottles of water are sold every minute. In areas without ready access to drinking water, these containers are lifesaving. That's not the case here, or in other First World countries. In the United States, less than 30 percent of the 38 million plastic bottles used each year ever get recycled. Worldwide, that number drops to a paltry 9 percent.

Food Waste

While eliminating as much plastic waste as possible is the most *urgent* goal of zero-waste programs, food waste is another big issue that needs to be addressed. The amount of wasted food in the United States alone is staggering: About 50 percent of all produce grown in the United States each year is thrown away—60 million tons' worth. This is about one-third of all the food we produce annually. And yet, people still go hungry in this country every day.

It is this food that, according to the EPA, takes up the greatest amount of space in our landfills, rotting in plastic garbage bags that can take decades or

BUY PRODUCE WITHOUT BAGS!

Yup, you can do this. You're going to wash the food when you get home anyway, so why add another bag? For the small stuff like mushrooms or green beans, use your leftover nonrecyclable plastic bags or reusable plastic containers. You can also try paper bags, which some stores are putting out now in the produce section. Companies like Eco-Bags Products sell smaller reusable bags in sets.

even centuries to decompose. This is a particularly bad outcome considering food waste is the most readily compostable material in our lives.

Getting Ugly

A major contributor to food waste is our national obsession with appearances. We want our produce to look magazine-perfect, even though that expectation is unrealistic when applied to nature's bounty.

What happens is that as soon as an apple gets a bruise, a banana shows a brown spot, or a head of lettuce gets a bit wilted, we toss it in the trash. We do this because food is so cheap in the United States thanks to government subsidies, which allow us to be the pickiest eaters on the planet. Too often we are not throwing away food because it's spoiled; we're throwing it away because it no longer looks pretty.

We need to change our thinking surrounding what constitutes "healthy" food by paying more attention to the nutritive value of foods and less attention to how they look. With this attitude, we can be less wasteful while also decreasing the demand for chemicals that are used simply to improve an edible's photogenic qualities. There are even some food box companies like Imperfect Foods and Misfits Market that specialize in delivering nutritious, delicious food that might not be considered "beautiful."

Helping the Homeless

The majority of food that gets thrown away is simply ugly (as we discussed), prepared in excess, not easily stored, or just plain unwanted. There are better uses for edible food in our country, starting with feeding the hungry and homeless. What do you have in your own pantry that you might consider donating to a food bank instead of letting it expire and then tossing it in the garbage?

The US Department of Agriculture's (USDA) website lists dozens of national organizations that recover and redistribute food from farmers, businesses, restaurants,

---

DEFINE YOUR TERMS

Zero waste: This is a philosophy and a set of principles that aim for a completely recyclable, no-trash cycle of production and consumption. The goal is to keep materials out of landfills, incinerators, and oceans. Renewable energy and biodegradable packaging are at the forefront of this movement.

GOOD GROCERY HABITS

In addition to cutting down on food waste, there are some good grocery habits you can get into that will help the environment in other ways.

Buy Produce in Season

Seasonal produce is usually more local than that offered out of season. Nearly all out-of-season produce is imported from foreign countries, particularly South America. Much of this produce is grown on land that was formerly Amazon rain forest, which has been burned and clear-cut for farming. While strawberries in winter and avocados year-round are wonderful, the environmental impacts of unsustainable farming practices have been catastrophic in countries such as Chile, Peru, and Mexico. A quick online search will help you find out what's seasonal when in your area.

Become Vegan or Vegetarian

The benefits of a plant-based diet are not just about improving our personal health (for which there is a lot of evidence), but also about decreasing the enormous impact of livestock farming.

Veganism avoids all animal products, including dairy, eggs, honey, and leather. Vegetarianism generally restricts meat consumption, but not all animal products. There are a number of "types" of vegetarians, so explore what appeals to you.

and schools across the country. The food produced in restaurants is high quality, but perishable. Getting this food to those in need requires special handling and rapid distribution, which costs a bit more, but it's being done every day. You can ask around in your own community to find out if food waste is being redistributed, and if it's not, you might be able to help local businesses and schools take initiative to change this.

Understanding Expiration Dates

Figuring out what to do with food waste is important, but even better is cutting down on the waste itself. There are a number of ways to decrease food waste in our country. One way is to commit ourselves to understanding what expiration dates really mean. For example, while most dairy products have extremely short expiration dates, those dates are set so that grocery stores have adequate time to pull the products from shelves before they spoil. *The dates do not reflect when the food actually becomes spoiled.* Spoilage depends on storage conditions and potential contamination opportunities. If a container of sour cream is stored in the refrigerator and seldom used, it will last for weeks past its "expiration" date; as long as the product isn't separated or smelly, it's likely safe to eat.

Buying in Bulk

When it comes to foods you know you're going to eat, the best way to buy them for both the environment and your wallet is in bulk. Many grocery stores allow you to buy in bulk from large, self-serve bins, and often you can even bring your own containers. But don't feel like you need to purchase special containers to hold your bulk food purchases. A nifty trick is to reuse containers from previously purchased foods to hold

bulk-bought versions of the same food. For example, use an empty coffee can or plastic jug to hold bulk coffee beans or ground coffee. The container has already been created specifically to hold that particular product, so the environment is getting twice the bang for your buck by keeping the empty container out of the landfill and reusing it to hold more of the same product. You don't even have to relabel it! Nuts, beans, spices, candy, snacks, and many other goods can all be stored this way.

Composting

A terrific way to use food waste is home composting. Composting breaks down organic materials by using natural organisms, such as worms, insects, and soil bacteria. Creating compost for your garden isn't difficult, but it requires an adjustment in thinking. By saving vegetable and fruit peelings, overripe produce, and stale or moldy breads and cereals, we can create a rich organic soil amendment that improves the texture, nutrient value, and water-holding capacity of our gardens and container plants. This is a free source of plant food that helps make even the poorest soils better.

Worms are always a big hit, especially with kids. "Red wigglers" are perfect for occupying indoor compost bins (excellent if you have no yard space) and quickly devour kitchen scraps, turning them into beautiful black "castings" (worm poop) that veggies can't get enough of.

You can buy worms and compost bins online for indoor use, but worms are wonderful in outdoor gardens as well. For outdoors, stick with good old earthworms, which are bigger and hardier for outdoor conditions. Worms are commonly sold as fishing bait all over the United States; alternatively, you can dig up a shovelful or two of soil from the worm-filled garden of a friend (with permission, of course) and

scatter it in your garden patch. By next year, the worms will have multiplied.

Shopping for Products

As much as we over-shop for food, we over-shop for stuff. We talked about secondhand shopping as a green way to get what you need in chapter 1, but we all realize that shopping is a national obsession and a driver of our economy. Eliminating it altogether is not going to be practical in our lifetimes. The most impactful way to shrink your ecological footprint is to change not only *what* you buy but also the *way* you buy it so as to cut down on waste. Shopping for personal care products is a good example.

WHAT *CAN'T* YOU COMPOST?

Do *not* compost meat and dairy products. Meat and dairy waste will attract scavenging animals to the compost pile; they'll tear it apart and will take advantage of whatever other food resources are in your yard, including digging up the garden, eating food put out for pets, and possibly harming the pets themselves. You also should not compost droppings from carnivorous pets, like dogs and cats, but you can compost the waste from herbivorous pets, such as rabbits and hamsters.

So many of the products produced for personal care (including shampoos and conditioners, deodorants, cosmetics, and skin care items) are overpackaged in single-use plastic. An example is disposable razors: They are made of nonbiodegradable plastic and can't be recycled due to the combination of plastic and metal in the product. An alternative to disposable razors is to use an electric shaver or to switch to a safety razor with a replaceable blade. (Safety razors are easier for men to use than for women because men are generally shaving a small area with a relatively flat surface, i.e., the face.)

A number of major cosmetic companies are starting to produce more environmentally conscious packaging for their products, including refillable inserts for soaps and creams, recyclable glass jars, and combination products that multitask so we don't have to buy as many different products in the first place. Some manufacturers even accept returns of the bottles and jars at their retail stores. For instance, The Body Shop has a recycling program for all of its containers. There are also numerous specialty manufacturers (including The Honest Company, Ilia, and Antonym Cosmetics) that create zero-waste products.

Pick Out Good Packaging

A major problem surrounding the many things we purchase is the issue of excessive packaging. Have you ever spent 10 minutes helping a kid remove a doll from its outer and inner boxes, only to discover that the doll is still strapped to yet more cardboard with twist ties and more plastic strips? This is an example of overpackaging, something manufacturers do to enhance how their products *look* rather than how they function. That doll looks more enticing with her hair spread out around her head and her accessories visibly arrayed like satellites. We can have an impact on pollution and the overload in our landfills

---

SWAP, DON'T SHOP!

Secondhand shopping (e.g., thrift stores and swap meets) can be an easy step toward living a zero-waste lifestyle. Yes, the products you buy were likely to have been manufactured in unsustainable ways or from materials that aren't considered *green*, but by reusing these products you're keeping them out of landfills and not contributing to the increased production of more of these same things. See the Reduce section on page 10 for more information.

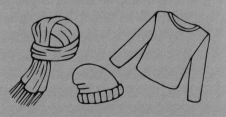

THE BIGGER THE BETTER!

Buy the largest version of the product you can. For example, soaps, detergents, oils, and vinegar often come in huge containers that you can use to refill smaller, easier-to-handle containers as needed. In addition, buying big packages means you don't have to shop as often, which saves trips to the store; you also typically save quite a bit of money on the larger sizes, ounce for ounce. This is also a good strategy if your local store doesn't offer bulk bins of dry goods.

by complaining to manufacturers about excessive packaging, and then buying from those that listen.

Delivery Issues

The development of next-day, to-door delivery has created a whole new group of problems that many people aren't aware of. For example, how many deliveries do you get in a day and from how many different companies? Each of those deliveries requires its own packaging to hold the different products, and they frequently utilize different delivery companies that all make multiple stops. How many extra boxes are you getting? What's happening to all that cardboard—and where is it coming from in the first place?

Overnight delivery relies on more aircraft delivery than over-the-road (OTR) shipping; airplanes are the most polluting form of transportation due to their relatively small carrying capacity and fuel inefficiency. The pollution generated is delivered straight to the upper atmosphere, where it increases the amount of greenhouse gases and contributes to global warming.

The amount of gas we save in getting delivery is dwarfed by the resulting amount used by delivery vehicles. Our convenience costs us more packaging waste for landfills, more deforestation to make shipping boxes, and billions of dollars in infrastructure to support delivery traffic—not to mention air pollution from more vehicles on the road and greater demand for fossil fuels. Limiting your use of to-door delivery of products you could find in stores is one of the best and easiest things you can do to reduce waste in a variety of ways all at once.

✳ ✳ ✳

Actions You Can Take

SEED

Practice refill-ability. Get a reusable water bottle and refill as needed. Or you can purchase a refillable beverage cup from the convenience store and buy a drink from the fountain instead of grabbing a plastic bottle of soda. Plastic straws can be rinsed and reused (really!), or you can buy stainless-steel straws or glass reusable straws instead. Try to avoid individually wrapped candies, snacks, drinks, and medicines. Using refillable shopping bags is one of the simplest steps to decrease the amount of plastic we produce as a nation.

SPROUT

Consider the packaging and buy in bulk. In addition to carrying reusable shopping totes, we can make better decisions about product packaging:

- Seek out products with the simplest packaging.
- Look for recyclable or biodegradable packaging and buy from manufacturers that use it.
- Buy food staples in bulk from stores like Whole Foods Market or Trader Joe's. Using your own refillable containers at these stores is an even bigger step toward a zero-waste lifestyle.

TREE

Remove single-use products from your life. Eliminate single-use plastics from your life. Avoid foods that come in plastic packaging and instead grow your own fruits and vegetables—and then use the food waste to create your own closed system with a compost pile.

- 3 -

Sustainability

The idea behind a "sustainable" lifestyle is to encourage production and consumption that minimize the environmental damage done to the Earth, while also leaving adequate resources for future generations to use and enjoy. Whereas most of what we've covered so far is about reducing waste and what goes into landfills, now we'll focus on how to pick products that are sustainable in terms of what they're made out of and how they're made.

The Need to Sustain

Why is sustainability so important? Right now, the human population is continuing to grow at a rate never before seen in our evolution. Better medical treatment, healthier living conditions, clean water, and reliable food sources are enabling us to reproduce faster and to have more children survive past infancy. We're also living a lot longer than we used to.

As the population grows, it puts more and more strain on the Earth's resources to provide for our needs. More people need more food to eat, more water to drink, more places to live. We build homes on land in the United States that's some of the richest farmland in the world—which decreases the availability of that land to grow food.

We spread out into areas that are ill-suited for human habitation (e.g., mountainsides, floodplains, and forests), leading to inevitable natural disasters such as mudslides due to clearing the hillsides of the trees that used to hold the soil in place. Barrier islands that once sheltered shorelines from heavy tides and hurricanes now have houses on them, which are destroyed when the next big hurricane comes. Afterward, we rebuild in the same places, costing taxpayers billions of dollars. We need to focus on sustainable practices for the production of goods and foods as well as where we live if we want the Earth to continue to be able to provide for us.

Zero Waste vs. Sustainability

Zero waste and sustainability have similar goals, but the approach is a bit different. Zero waste seeks to minimize trash output, but doesn't necessarily focus on responsible

DEFINE YOUR TERMS

Sustainable: This refers to methods and practices that can be continued at a particular rate without depleting natural resources. For example, **sustainable agriculture** uses farming practices that don't break down or impoverish soils, contaminate water, or kill beneficial insects such as bees. **Sustainable forestry** doesn't clear-cut timber but instead selectively harvests older trees so that younger ones can grow up and take their places. A crop like bamboo can be a sustainable resource because it grows fast enough to keep up with a high rate of harvest.

manufacturing. An example in chapter 2 was switching to a vegetarian diet: While eating more fruits and vegetables is good for our health, our desire for variety leads to us buying nonseasonal and exotic produce that can sap water resources and destroy faraway forests. These kinds of side effects are what sustainability seeks to avoid.

Next, we'll look at some of the ways adopting sustainable practices will contribute to a better, greener world.

Sustainable Agriculture

Beginning the discussion with sustainable agriculture makes sense: We all need to eat to live. Sustainable farming isn't new. Prior to the Industrial Revolution, most farming was organic and sustainable because farmers didn't have access to chemical pesticides. They had to use animal waste and bioorganic compost to fertilize crops. They also had to adopt techniques that preserved soil integrity and its ability to consistently produce. Failure to follow such practices could result in crop failure and famine that affected hundreds or thousands of people.

Sustainable farming today faces many concerns: water conservation, soil preservation, profit and yield, investment costs, economic forces, environmental impacts, long-term viability, and more. Let's look at a few of these.

Profitability

In our current capitalistic economy, money makes the world go round. Without profits, farmers aren't going to be able to adopt or maintain newer practices with lower environmental impact. Investments in more fuel-efficient equipment, hardier seed and breed stock, and data mining software that can monitor improvements in yield and crop loss are all going to be borne up front by the farmers themselves. It's going to take a couple of harvests before those costs can be passed on to consumers—and even then, most farmers won't recoup all of those investments.

What's needed are ways to reduce those up-front costs; co-ops, venture capital groups, and national governments are going to have to figure out how to help farmers make the shift to sustainable practices.

Farmers' Quality of Life

Maintaining quality of life for farming families and communities is a major concern with the rise of "factory farms," where corporations buy up small farms and consolidate them into giant conglomerates. This destroys the ability of small farmers to make a living and support local communities. It also leads to profit being the primary concern, at the expense of resource management and humane animal husbandry in an industry that is ecologically harmful.

Resource Conservation

We can't grow enough crops to feed us all without soil and water resources. Soil conservation, water management, and agricultural pollution are all important parts of sustainable agriculture. The widespread use of damaging pesticides impacts both native

plants and beneficial insect populations. It is damage from some of these pesticides that is believed to be responsible for the worldwide decline of bees, which are vital to the pollination of many fruit and vegetable crops. Farmers use pesticides to prevent predation by insects (which reduces yield) and improve the "beauty" of the produce. By accepting some blemishes, we can help encourage the reduction of pesticides, which can help farmers save money in bringing their crops to market.

Each year, the Environmental Working Group comes out with the Clean Fifteen and Dirty Dozen lists to tell people the kinds of produce that tests show have the least and most pesticides. For more on these lists, see pages 115 and 116.

Soil

Soil is the basis of all agriculture; it supports crop growth for humans and livestock alike, filters precipitation into underground aquifers where water can be drawn out, and sustains the teeming mass of plant and animal life across the globe. Though most of us do not have to worry about soil in our day-to-day life (unless we're gardeners or farmers), learning about the harmful effect that ecologically unsustainable farming practices have on the environment around us is a valuable piece of knowledge for any person trying to live greener.

Soil is quite fragile. Its structure is complex and not all soils are suitable for growing crops. Most native plants have adapted to the different soil types around the world and are perfectly suited for the site. Therefore, the process of clearing forests to grow crops causes a number of problems, such as soil erosion, low yields,

BIG NUMBERS Soil erosion is occurring at such an alarming rate that scientists estimate current crop yields could be cut in half over the next 30 to 50 years. Decreasing yields by 50 percent would bring famine to areas that currently don't have it, and wipe out the population in areas that do.

and poor fertility. In fact, fertility in tropical areas tends to be so poor that the cleared patch of land is no longer able to support crop growth after just a couple of seasons, so a new patch is cleared and the problem spreads.

Soil erosion is the primary cause of mudslides. As tree and native plant cover on slopes is decreased (whether from development, clear-cutting, or die-off), the plant roots that used to hold the thin soils on the hillsides also die. Without the roots

BUY LOCAL EVERYWHERE!

While farmers' markets and CSAs are ideal for bulk buying, not everyone has access to them. When you're at the grocery store, take a look at produce labels. If a sign indicates that the red raspberries are local and the blackberries are from another state, consider buying the red raspberries instead. This saves fuel emissions and transportation waste. Buying locally grown, in-season produce helps decrease the demand for exotic fruits, which in turn discourages slash-and-burn agricultural practices on land not suited for it.

holding it in place, the soil becomes too heavy when waterlogged with rain. The top water-soaked layers slide off, often taking underlying rocks with them, and the result is a "natural" disaster with catastrophic damage. Preventing soil erosion and preserving the structure of soils is an important environmental issue. Ask anyone in California or Washington State about mudslides.

One more important consideration in protecting soil integrity is the storage of atmospheric carbons. Soils contain more stored carbon than all of the land plants and the entire atmosphere combined, through a process known as *biosequestration*. In the evergreen forests of Canada, for example, as much as 80 percent of total carbon is stored in the organic portion of the soil. Soil erosion exposes organic matter to environmental degradation, which releases the carbon from the materials and allows

it to reenter the atmosphere. There, it combines with oxygen to make carbon dioxide (CO_2), a potent greenhouse gas. Greenhouse gases contribute to global warming, and global warming contributes to climate change. We need to discourage widespread deforestation to prevent the release of this stored carbon into the atmosphere. This is an enormous task, but there are some ways we can all help.

What's Up with GMOs?

Another matter of concern in sustainable agriculture is genetically modified organisms (GMOs). These animals (mainly dairy cattle, so far) and plants have undergone gene-splicing procedures to create features and characteristics that do not naturally occur in the organism. Corn and soybeans are the most common GMOs in the United

---

DEFINE YOUR TERMS

Deforestation: The loss of tree cover from a given area is called deforestation. Loss may be due to timber cutting, land clearing for farming or development, or even soil erosion or climate change. Loss of trees is a critical environmental concern because trees are one of the biggest absorbers of carbon dioxide (CO_2) from the atmosphere. Trees and other plants use CO_2 for photosynthesis and release oxygen as a by-product. Deforestation is heaviest in tropical forests, with only 2.4 million square miles remaining of the 6 million square miles that once covered Earth's surface. A football field–size area is cleared from the Amazon rain forest every minute.

A GMO WORLD

The question is: What happens to the modified genes in the wild? There's no reason to assume that spliced genes are not passed on to the next generation when plants interbreed. These modified genes are then passed on again and again, until plants that formerly had no genetically modified components now contain them. But their products don't get labeled "genetically modified" because the parent plant came from wild populations. It's already been proven in corn plants that non-GMO plants can become contaminated by contact with GMO plants.

Furthermore, if livestock are eating GMO corn and soy, and then humans eat the meat and dairy produced by the livestock, humans are being exposed to GMOs even if the animal itself hasn't been genetically modified. The corn *becomes* the cow. There is ample evidence showing that pesticide residues that dairy cattle are exposed to are detectable in their milk. Whether the cows eat pesticide-treated plants, inhale pesticide drift from the air, or consume plants that have pesticides spliced into them, the fact remains that pesticides are transmitted in the milk those cows produce.

Fortunately for the organic movement, preventive programs are being launched. For example, the voluntary organic registry website at Purdue University known as DriftWatch is a communication tool that enables crop producers, beekeepers, and pesticide applicators to work together to protect specialty crops and apiaries through computer mapping programs. Currently, 12 states are participating.

States; a whopping 93 percent of corn and soy produced in this country has been genetically modified, usually for resistance to herbicides such as glyphosate (trade named Roundup) or to introduce pesticides directly into the plant so that it doesn't need additional spraying. Most of this corn and soy winds up as livestock feed, biodiesel fuel—and *corn syrup*. Corn syrup (especially high-fructose corn syrup) is a sweetener present in nearly all snack foods and beverages, as well as condiments, baby food, and between 60 and 70 percent of all other grocery store foods. Other GMOs include sugar beets, canola oil, and cotton.

One of the gravest concerns of genetically modified organisms is how they affect the normal species in the environment. A lot of cross-pollination occurs between plants of the same species: Nearly all *Zea mays* (corn) plants can crossbreed with each other, as can tomatoes, potatoes, apples, and other crop species. In fact, many fruits require cross-pollination by a *different* species of the same fruit to provide the largest and best-quality crop: Apples, cherries, blueberries, hazelnuts, pistachios, and almonds all require or perform better with cross-pollination.

Some major agricultural companies have taken pains to create seeds that are *sterile*. In other words, you can't grow a new crop by planting seeds harvested from the previous crop. This greatly benefits the agricultural company because farmers are forced to buy new seed from the company every year to produce a crop. This manipulation is highly detrimental to crops because it decreases genetic diversity in the species, making it much more subject to failure from disease, insect predation, and environmental stresses. This is why manufacturers splice pesticides into their products in the first place: because

they know that the crop is weaker than a crop grown by natural means.

Sustainable Manufacturing

In discussing green manufacturing, we have to look at not just the energy sources used to produce goods, but also the materials and practices. Materials such as steel, aluminum, and glass can be recycled almost indefinitely, but the *raw* materials needed to create those things (iron and aluminum ores, silica, etc.) are finite. Eventually, there will be no more metals to mine. Minimizing natural resource use, recycling and reusing what was once considered waste, and

WHO'S USING WHAT

Here's a breakdown of what percentage each economic sector in the United States is contributing toward our total emissions. Manufacturing produces 26.6%, and moving to sustainable practices can cut that way down.

Transportation
- Road transport (10.5%)
- Air transport (excluding additional warming impacts) (1.7%)
- Other transport (2.5%)

Energy
- Fuel and power for residential buildings (10.2%)
- Fuel and power for commercial buildings (6.3%)
- Unallocated fuel combustion (3.8%)

Manufacturing
- Iron and steel production (4%)
- Aluminum and non-ferrous metals production (1.2%)
- Machinery production (1%)
- Pulp, paper, and printing (1.1%)
- Food and tobacco industries (1.0%)
- Chemicals production (4.1%)
- Cement production (5.0%)
- Other industry (7.0%)
- Transmission and distribution losses (2.2%)

Land-Use Changes
- Coal mining (1.3%)
- Oil and gas production (6.4%)
- Deforestation (11.3%)
- Reforestation (–0.4%)

Agriculture
- Harvest and land management (1.3%)
- Agricultural energy use (1.4%)
- Agricultural soils (5.2%)
- Livestock and manure (5.4%)
- Rice cultivation (1.5%)
- Other cultivation (1.7%)
- Landfill waste (1.7%)
- Wastewater and other waste (1.5%)

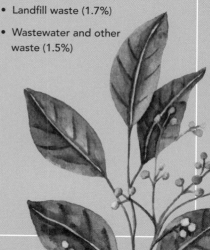

reducing emissions are all important considerations for making manufacturing of all types more sustainable.

What does this mean for us as individuals? It's important for us to recognize and own our power to influence government and business decisions. For example, American auto manufacturing is making a concerted effort to move its business model toward the manufacture of green vehicles—specifically, electric-powered. As US government administrations come and go, the mandate to make such changes also fluctuates, so it's actually new, younger car buyers driving this change. They want energy-efficient vehicles, and they want those vehicles to be nonpolluting. The only energy source we currently have that is capable of delivering the performance level of gasoline-powered vehicles is electric, so the industry finds itself moving in that direction.

The choices we make as consumers every day have the power to effect change from the top down. Manufacturers create more of what we want to buy, even if it takes them a while to recognize new paradigms.

The United States remains the largest manufacturing economy in the world, supplying more than 20 percent of all manufactured goods. Allowing this productive capacity to die would be devastating to the economies of many of the world's nations, but that doesn't mean it can't be improved upon.

While antiquated manufacturing techniques dating from the mid-20th century are still in use in some sectors, growing numbers of businesses are finding that adopting newer green manufacturing practices not only improves the bottom line, but also increases employee motivation, morale, and positive public relations.

With this in mind, new manufacturing paradigms are emerging. For instance, so-called "cradle-to-cradle" manufacturing calls for products to be designed, produced, and distributed with the goal of eliminating (or at least *minimizing*) resource use, waste, and pollution. Included are considerations of how the product will be disposed of at the end of its life (such as the potential for reuse or recycling).

Start-up companies and some traditional manufacturers are looking at many different ways we can continue to feed, clothe, and house the increasing world population. Let's look at some alternatives to standard manufacturing.

PAY IT FORWARD!

Buy from companies that use sustainable manufacturing practices and biodegradable packaging. Boycott those that don't.

BIG NUMBERS The fashion industry is a $3 trillion per year global industry, and the second-largest source of industrial pollution on the planet following the oil industry. Are you surprised? The global apparel and footwear manufacturing processes combined account for over 8 percent of the entire world's greenhouse gas emissions (including CO_2, methane, nitrous oxide, and fluorinated greenhouse gases)—in other words, almost as much as the total carbon impact of the entire European Union!

The apparel industry alone accounts for 6.7 percent of the world's greenhouse gas emissions, with more than 50 percent of those emissions coming from just three phases of manufacture: fiber production (15 percent), yarn preparation (28 percent), and the highest-impact phase—dyeing and finishing (36 percent). All of this to produce more than 150 billion garments annually—enough to provide 20 new garments to every person on the planet, every year.

It's not just greenhouse gas emissions that are a problem. One-quarter of the chemicals produced in the world are used in textiles. Nearly 70 million barrels of oil are used each year to make polyester fiber, now the most commonly used fiber in clothing in the world—but it takes more than 200 years for that fiber to decompose. Microfibers shed from synthetic clothing account for 85 percent of the microplastic contamination in the oceans. And garment manufacturing also contributes to global deforestation; more than 70 million trees are cut down each year and turned into fabrics like rayon and viscose and the lower-impact fibers modal and lyocell.

Textiles

Textile manufacturing has historically been one of the most environmentally damaging processes in the world. Huge amounts of clean water are needed to cull and clean the fiber (whether from plant, animal, or petroleum sources), spin and dye the yarn, weave the fabric (which may be bleached or dyed again), and, finally, create a garment. Not all of these steps necessarily take place in the same factory—or even the same country—which adds pollution due to transportation.

Without substantial changes in the manufacturing process, the impact of apparel manufacturing on the climate is expected to increase by 49 percent, which will be equal to the total annual greenhouse gas emissions of the United States in 2019.

Manufacturing practices aren't the only issue with the apparel industry. A lot of the fabric that is created never actually makes it into the final garment. Most major fashion companies—from fast fashion brands to *continued*

THE LOWDOWN ON ELECTRIC CARS

The world of electric cars is fairly new and always changing. Here are some of the biggest questions people have when they considering getting off the gas and going electric:

What's the Difference Between Electric and Hybrid Vehicles?

There are two types of electric vehicles (EVs), according to the US Office of Energy Efficiency and Renewable Energy: There are all-electric vehicles (AEVs), which have electric motors instead of internal combustion engines and are completely powered by electricity. There are also plug-in hybrid electric vehicles (PHEVs), which have internal combustion engines as well as electric motors. PHEVs need to be both filled up with gasoline and charged via electricity. That means they get some of their power from gasoline and some from the electric motor.

Then as a bonus item, there are hybrid cars. Hybrids need to be filled with gas just like conventional cars, but they cannot be plugged in to be charged. They generate some electric power via regenerative braking, meaning they need to get gas less often than gas-powered cars.

Do Electric Vehicles Save You Money?

Buying an electric car means you'll never have to fill up your car with gas again—which means you'll save money on gas. According to a 2018 University of Michigan study, the average price to power an EV each year is $485, while the average for a conventional, gasoline-powered car is $1,117.

All-electric vehicles and hybrid cars also almost always have lower maintenance costs than gas-powered cars. That's because internal combustion engines come with a slew of equipment that tends to need repairs, such as transmissions, exhausts, and spark plugs; additionally, EVs have regenerative brakes that are powered by electric motors, which means brake pads and rotors do not need maintenance as often.

Plus, you can also save money thanks to various EV incentives and tax credits. In 2021, the US government gave EV drivers a tax credit for up to $7,500 for each new EV purchased, with the exact amount depending on the vehicle's size, battery, and so on. Additionally, some states and cities provide EV owners with other incentives, such as additional tax credits, rebates, loans, discounted charging rates, and permission to drive in the carpool lane (aka the high-occupancy vehicle lane) even if there aren't any additional passengers.

How Are Electric Vehicles Charged?

There are various ways to power electric vehicles. All-electric vehicles have batteries that need to be charged by plugging them into a charging station, which car owners do most frequently at home, as well as at public charging stations while on the go.

AEVs, PHEVs, and hybrid cars can also charge via regenerative braking, which happens when a driver brakes, either to stop, slow down, or while driving downhill. Braking stores kinetic energy in a car's battery, and then uses that stored energy to send power back to the car's wheels, as explained by the website Explain That Stuff.

How Often Do You Have to Charge Electric Vehicles?

Each EV is different, meaning the amount of driving time one charge will give you varies greatly from car to car. According to the Plug-In Hybrid & Electric Vehicle Research Center at UC Davis cars can take anywhere from 20 minutes to 20 hours to get a charge of 80 percent to 100 percent, depending on the type of battery in the car, and what type of charger is used. A full charge will give most EV drivers about 100 miles of driving, except for certain models, like the Tesla Model S, which can drive 350 miles on a full charge, as per the research center.

For most EV drivers, charging overnight at home or while parked at work is enough to sustain their commute and day-to-day activities. But EV drivers going on road trips or driving more than a few hours at a time will need to find charging stations along their route.

Do Electric Vehicles Produce Emissions?

EVs are much more environmentally friendly than gas-powered cars, but they do still produce emissions. According to the Alternative Fuels Data Center, annual average emissions for each kind of car in the United States are as follows:

- All electric: 4,352 pounds of CO_2 equivalent
- Plug-in hybrid: 6,044 pounds of CO_2 equivalent
- Hybrid: 6,258 pounds of CO_2 equivalent
- Gasoline: 11,435 pounds of CO_2 equivalent

So, not only is the price of powering an EV less than half powering a gas-powered car, but it also usually produces less than half the emissions.

Are Electric Vehicles Good for the Environment?

Wait, but doesn't all that electric energy being used to power electric vehicles come from fossil fuels?! At the moment, most of it does. However, the US electricity grid is constantly shifting toward renewable energy (including solar power, wind power, and hydropower). The more that renewable energy powers the US grid, the more environmentally friendly EVs become.

designer labels—design patterns that do not use entire rectangles of fabric, leaving a ton of scraps (known as deadstock and offcuts) to be sent to landfills. And some companies take that level of waste a step further by incinerating perfectly good clothing that they are unable to sell. For example, fashion house Burberry made headlines for incinerating $36.5 million worth of new clothing in the year 2017, which, according to the *New York Post*, the brand reportedly did to prevent the clothing from hitting the market at discounted prices.

We can use our power as consumers to force changes in the way garment manufacturers create their apparel. Every purchase we make from companies that use sustainable practices increases the demand for eco-friendly fashion. Also, since there is already a significant surplus of clothes in existence, we don't actually *need* that many new clothes to be produced—meaning that the pressure for fashion brands to be considered sustainable keeps rising.

Practice Slow Fashion

Even though fast fashion's price tags are usually low, the cost to the environment and to the people making the clothing is often high—not to mention, the low price tag isn't actually as low as it appears. That $5 T-shirt most likely will not last very long, making it essentially a disposable item in the eyes of many consumers—which keeps them coming back to the store for yet more replacements.

Common fast fashion shops and online stores include Forever 21, Nasty Gal, Zara, Gap, Primark, Uniqlo, Topshop, Urban Outfitters, and H&M. If you want to avoid supporting fast fashion products, stay away from any shop where the prices seem way too good to be true, or where new styles are appearing daily or weekly on shelves.

There are many designers combating fast fashion with ethical, sustainable, and slow fashion practices. Smaller fashion labels, including Tonlé and Zero Waste Daniel, use deadstock fabric or preconsumer fabric waste to make their clothes, meaning they do not produce any waste. Many larger fashion designers and brands have dedicated their businesses to low-waste, ethical, and sustainable practices, including Eileen Fisher, Stella McCartney, and Reformation.

Brands that utilize sustainable business practices do not cut the same corners that fast fashion brands do. Unfortunately, the price of fair labor practices and sustainability initiatives is often higher than outsourcing to sweatshops that underpay their employees. So, even though some sustainable fashion brands are pricey, think of buying a responsibly made garment as an up-front investment, since the item could last for many years.

If you want to learn more about sustainable fashion (and there is so much to learn), there are many bloggers and YouTubers you can use as resources for

BIG NUMBERS Cotton is the world's most chemically demanding crop, using 24 percent of all insecticides and 11 percent of all pesticides globally. This dependency on chemical sprays contaminates both soil and water, leading to the leaching of pesticides into rivers and aquifers, and eventually into the oceans. Cotton is also a very thirsty crop: It takes 5,284 gallons of water to grow enough cotton to make one T-shirt and one pair of jeans.

brand recommendations, tips, donation advice, and more. Some knowledgeable ethical fashion bloggers include *EcoCult*, *The Un-Material Girl*, *Old World New*, *Adimay*, and *Sutton + Grove*.

Microfibers

In chapter 2, we looked at the problem with microplastics in the environment. Now let's consider the impact of microfibers from textiles. When any fabric rolls around in the washing machine it sheds microfibers, which are tiny fibers less than 10 micrometers in diameter—about one-fifth the diameter of a human hair. This is only a concern when washing fabric made from synthetic materials (such as polyester, nylon, spandex, and rayon), which will never break down (unlike fibers from natural materials such as cotton, linen, and bamboo).

ONLY SPECIAL DELIVERIES!

Avoid daily and overnight delivery of goods. These products, while cheap and convenient, increase airplane traffic, clog streets with gas-guzzling delivery vehicles, and create tremendous amounts of cardboard and other shipping waste.

IN GOOD COMPANY

When we embrace sustainable practices such as thrift shopping (which keeps clothing, accessories, and jewelry out of landfills and gives them a second or third life), we help eliminate the use of resources that would otherwise be required to make new products. If you have local thrift, consignment, secondhand, and vintage stores, those are the best places to go because the clothing didn't have to travel far to get there, but there are also some great online shops:

Goodwill is a national nonprofit that uses the money it earns from selling secondhand donations to help train and place people in jobs. It has online auctions with a wide variety of goods and clothing.

Poshmark is an online marketplace where you can sell and buy secondhand clothing and home goods.

Depop is an online marketplace that focuses on fashion and unique items.

ThredUP offers high-quality secondhand clothing sold on consignment.

eBay is the original online auction site, though not everything on there is secondhand these days.

Rent the Runway allows you to rent high fashion items, which means pieces like gowns and other formal attire will get worn again and again instead of costing a fortune to be worn only once and then left to languish in your closet.

One Warm Coat knows that a quality coat that'll keep you warm and protect you from the elements could cost a pretty penny—making it a necessity that many Americans can't afford. This organization is helping make sure that money isn't a factor in staying warm during the winter by outfitting adults and children in need with coats provided by donations. Since its inception in 1992, it has given more than 5 million coats to those in need in the United States and 10 other countries, thanks to more than 31,000 coat drives held so far. As One Warm Coat explains on its site, "Health experts report that even a 2-degree drop in body temperature results in reduced heart rate, loss of coordination, and confusion. Adults cannot work effectively, and children find it difficult to learn."

MINIMIZE YOUR MICROFIBERS

There are a variety of ways to lower the number of microfibers your laundry cycle releases. According to the Plastic Pollution Coalition, you can

- run loads as full as possible (full loads cause less friction and fewer microfibers to shed).

- wash with cold water, which encourages fewer microfibers to release and uses less energy.

- wear clothing made from natural materials instead of synthetics.

- wash your clothing less often.

- use a wash bag made to capture microfibers in the washing machine.

- use a Cora Ball when you do laundry to help prevent microfibers from breaking off in the first place and collect the ones that do so that you can put them in the trash instead of letting them go into the water system.

Synthetic microfibers are a kind of microplastic—so when these tiny fibers shed in the machine, they enter the water pipes and flow to waterways like oceans and rivers. Once there, they become plastic pollution, and are often consumed by fish and other sea animals. An estimated 100,000 synthetic microfibers are shed during every wash cycle, according to *Wired* magazine.

Sustainable Materials

One important avenue of investigation into mitigating the damage caused by the textile industry is the potential for using *nontraditional* plant fibers. The amount of energy used to produce the fiber is another consideration in the environmental impact made by the clothing industry.

- **Linen** is a natural material, woven from the fibers of the flax plant (a member of the family that includes hemp and jute). The energy requirement of linen is the lowest of any of the fiber sources.

- **Hemp** is a seldom-used fiber in modern times, but historically, this plant was critical in the making of ropes, sacks, and rough clothing—and was one of the most important crops to farmers in the American colonies. There is a recent push to lift the ban on growing hemp, a close relative of marijuana, in the United States. Hemp is a low water-use plant that doesn't require any spraying, provides large harvests, is incredibly tough and durable, and thrives in hot, difficult growing conditions.

- **Bamboo**, a member of the grass family, has been used to make everything from flooring to clothing, and its pulp can be made into paper. It grows extremely fast, is insect-free, and colonizes readily. The same patch of bamboo can be reharvested every few years, making bamboo cheap and sustainable. Bamboo can be processed into two different types of fabrics: bamboo linen and bamboo rayon. Bamboo linen is made through pulping the wood and spinning the fiber into yarn to be woven, whereas bamboo rayon goes through a more chemically intense process. Bamboo fabrics are great for products that see heavy use, including towels, clothing, and bedding.

- **New fabrics** are also being created from plant materials: Tencel, maker of **lyocell** and **modal fibers**, uses sustainably produced raw wood and environmentally responsible processes to create its products. Tencel's Refibra manufacturing process recycles cotton scrap fabric and wood pulp to make new lyocell fabric for clothing manufacturers such as H&M, Ted Baker London, J.Crew, Esprit, Victoria's Secret, Levi's, and more than a hundred others.

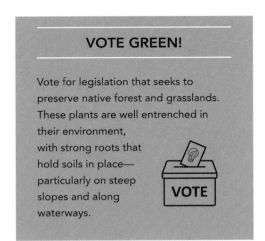

VOTE GREEN!

Vote for legislation that seeks to preserve native forest and grasslands. These plants are well entrenched in their environment, with strong roots that hold soils in place— particularly on steep slopes and along waterways.

VOTE

Sustainable Development

At the beginning of this chapter, we touched on the idea of how human population growth puts pressure not only on natural resources but also on wildlife. Land use for human housing and food production is the most critical issue that wildlife faces. As humans expand across the landscape, we not only physically take up the spaces where animals previously lived, but we also dismantle the ecosystems that have supported them for millennia.

Wildlife, with no place left to go as we take more and more of their habitat, is pushing back. Skunks, raccoons, and opossums were once forest animals, but have adapted to city life over the past century. Urban deer are a problem for gardeners and drivers in most of the United States, while even our largest cities are now having encounters with black bears and mountain lions. Coyotes are becoming bold enough and hungry enough to snatch pet dogs right off their owners' leashes. We have to get better at sharing the land.

Sustainable development goes hand in hand with land-use planning, which is a political construct that determines how land can be altered for human use to maximize resource extraction and profit without degrading those resources or damaging the environment. And this doesn't just apply to housing. Development includes extractive industries, such as mining and logging, as well as building roads and cities for people. We need to start thinking sustainably in all these areas, because every bit of development we do costs us land that *cannot be turned back* to its wild state. Industry's attempts at "remediation" do not replicate the diversity that virgin land can support, and we cannot tear down a housing development and return it to the fertile farmland it once was.

Sustainable Living

So, what can we do as individuals? While the problems of sustainability seem overwhelming, there are many things we can do to encourage governments and businesses to adopt a sustainability mind-set.

Your Vote, Your Voice

Voting is the most straightforward—and one of the easiest—things we can all do to push our world toward sustainability. Whereas voting access is a problem in some areas of the world, in the United States this generally isn't the case. All that's required is to register and then show up at the right place.

It's easy nowadays to find information about where candidates stand on environmental issues. Major environmental organizations like the Sierra Club, the National Wildlife Federation, and the Nature Conservancy put out articles before primary elections that list the candidates with the best voting records on environmental issues. Take a little time to find out which candidates align with your personal beliefs, then support them at the polls. In this way, we can turn our governments from special interest machines into planetary stewards.

SUSTAINABILITY GOALS FROM THE U.N.

In 2015, the United Nations came up with 17 sustainable development goals it hopes to fully implement by 2030. Here are its goals:

1. No poverty—*End poverty in all its forms everywhere.* An estimated 783 million people around the world live in extreme poverty. Over half of the world's population has no social benefit protections.

2. Zero hunger—*End hunger, achieve food security and improved nutrition, and promote sustainable agriculture.* An estimated 700 million people on Earth are malnourished.

3. Good health and well-being—*Ensure healthy lives and promote well-being for all at all ages.* Major diseases such as tuberculosis and malaria are increasing, while at least half of the world's population lacks access to essential healthcare services.

4. Quality education—*Ensure inclusive and equitable quality education and promote lifelong learning opportunities for all.* Over 50 percent of school-aged children have not achieved minimum proficiency levels in reading and mathematics.

5. Gender equality—*Achieve gender equality and empower all women and girls.* Forty-nine countries around the world do not have laws protecting women and girls from physical and sexual violence. According to recent data from about 90 countries, women devote roughly three times more hours per day to *unpaid* care and domestic work than men. This limits women's availability for paid work while keeping them financially and educationally disadvantaged.

6. Clean water and sanitation—*Ensure availability and sustainable management of water and sanitation for all.* Despite improvements, poor economics and infrastructure issues mean that 3 in 10 people worldwide still do not having access to clean drinking water.

7. Affordable and clean energy—*Ensure access to affordable, reliable, sustainable, and modern energy for all.* An estimated 840 million people on Earth do not have access to modern electricity. And nonrenewable, environmentally damaging fossil fuels supply 80 percent of the world's energy needs.

8. Decent work and economic growth—*Promote sustained, inclusive, and sustainable economic growth, full and productive employment, and decent work for all.* The gross domestic product (GDP) per capita worldwide is not increasing, despite increases in labor productivity. The poor are staying poor while working harder.

9. Industries, innovation, and infrastructure—*Build resilient infrastructure, promote inclusive and sustainable industrialization, and foster innovation.* Critical concerns include transportation issues, manufacturing capacity, and investment dollars.

10. Reduced inequalities—*Reduce inequality within and among countries.* Children, women, racial and religious minorities, people with disabilities, and underdeveloped countries need more protections.

11. Sustainable cities and communities—*Make cities and human settlements inclusive, safe, resilient, and sustainable.* Cities and communities need to grow while respecting the environment—including arable land, natural resources, and climate.

12. Responsible consumption and production—*Ensure sustainable consumption and production patterns.* Rampant population growth and consumption seriously threaten the achievement of all other sustainable development goals. Worldwide material consumption has increased 254 percent since 1970, while world population has increased just 189 percent.

13. Climate action—*Take urgent action to combat climate change and its impacts.* Since the climate crisis is a global issue, developed nations around the world need to work together while assisting developing countries in mitigating climate damage.

14. Life below water—*Conserve and sustainably use the oceans, seas, and marine resources for sustainable development.* Ocean acidification has increased 26 percent since preindustrial times, and could reach 100 percent or more by the end of this century—destroying plant and animal life in the seas.

15. Life on land—*Protect, restore, and promote sustainable use of terrestrial ecosystems, sustainably manage forests, combat desertification, and halt and reverse land degradation and biodiversity loss.* From 2000 to 2015, more than one-fifth of the Earth's total land area was degraded, largely due to human-induced processes.

16. Peace, justice, and strong institutions—*Promote peaceful and inclusive societies for sustainable development, provide access to justice for all, and build effective, accountable, and inclusive institutions at all levels.* Reducing corruption, eliminating sexual violence and human trafficking, and protecting the lives of human rights defenders are among the most pressing issues.

17. Partnerships for the goals—*Strengthen the means of implementation and revitalize the global partnership for sustainable development.* Private financial interests conflict with many sustainable development goals; more international cooperation is needed to implement stated development goals.

Giving Green

Supporting nongovernmental organizations (NGOs) that have an environmental focus is another way to join sustainable communities. NGOs include national groups like the Sierra Club, the Environmental Working Group, the Audubon Society, and many others. Becoming a paying member of such groups is easy and can be fairly cheap. (The Sierra Club has memberships starting as low as $15 per year.) Your membership fee goes to support the group's work, and it will send you updates on what it's focused on and the progress it's making. Some groups also offer free swag when you join, though you can decline such offers if you wish.

Support charities and national groups that reclaim and reuse material goods and resources for those in need. But be aware that charities that take donations and sell them for cash can sometimes *contribute* to unsustainable practices. For instance, when a charity receives donations of clothing and goods that exceed its capacity to house and sell them all, the excess is frequently sold to wholesalers and scrappers that shred the goods to collect raw fibers or valuable metals. This does nothing to improve sustainability, because scrapped goods are replaced by newly purchased goods in the consumer stream. To avoid contributing to this, check to see what a charity's practices are before you donate money or goods to it.

When you're donating goods, it's best to support *local* charities and groups. By choosing local groups, you decrease transportation costs and the environmental impact created by moving goods around the country. This is especially important for donations of large items like furniture, appliances, and electronics. You also help distribute goods in areas that may not be served by centralized donation programs in major cities.

Sustainable Shopping

As we talked about in previous chapters, our consumption mind-set needs to change in a lot of ways. Before buying anything, decide what your true needs are: How many shirts and shoes do you really need? As we've already discussed, the fashion industry has an enormous negative impact on the environment. Meanwhile, it's been estimated that the average American regularly wears only about 30 percent of the clothing in their closets. *Thirty percent!* If we reduce our clothing purchases by half, we're consuming less resources and decreasing the demand for more production—production often done overseas by people paid substandard wages. These products subsequently consume fossil fuels to ship them to the United States and then move them to retail outlets (including Amazon).

IN GOOD COMPANY

In chapter 1 we listed a variety of groups that take in used goods and redistribute them to needy individuals and families. These three companies are some of the top local organizations in the United States:

Habitat for Humanity ReStore accepts a wide range of household goods, appliances, furniture, and building materials that will be used to build the homes it gives away. Some donations are sold in the ReStore and not redistributed directly.

Humane Society of America typically needs used blankets, towels, and sheets for animal bedding. Call your local shelter to see if it's accepting donations at present.

2ReWear collects clothing, footwear, and household textiles for reuse and recycling. It is the textile industry's most efficient postconsumer goods recycler, reclaiming more than 100 million pounds of textiles each year via a network of partners in 14 states.

DEFINE YOUR TERMS

Carbon footprint: This is the amount of carbon compounds (including carbon dioxide) produced by an individual or group as a result of consuming fossil fuels. So, the gas we put in our cars; the coal, oil, and natural gas we use directly to heat our homes; and the fossil fuels used by industry to manufacture our goods and transport them to us are all part of our individual carbon footprint. The average American is responsible for *16.4 metric tons* of CO_2 emissions per year. Nations have carbon footprints as well: The United States emits 16 percent of the world's carbon dioxide. Note that this term was created by an oil company to put the responsibility of pollution on the consumer instead of itself and other large polluters, so be on the lookout for when it's used to shift blame instead of actually help.

The best way to decrease demand in the market is to buy things used. Once you've decided what you really need, investigate secondhand sources. Thrift shopping has changed dramatically from the days of dim shops with musty offerings. Fine jewelry, high-end accessories, and designer labels are common in secondhand stores nowadays, alongside barely used sports equipment and crystal stemware. There's a secondhand source for practically anything you want to buy.

Many of the practices we've discussed, such as reducing, reusing, and recycling, are excellent for improving sustainability. When we think about adopting a sustainable lifestyle, we need to think about not only our immediate needs but also the long-term consequences of the choices we make. For example, when we choose locally grown produce, we are not only making healthier choices for ourselves and our families, but we're also decreasing our *carbon footprint*, which benefits future generations. Buying local goods supports community economies and encourages small businesses, which provide jobs for area residents.

When buying new, we have more choices than ever before when it comes to purchasing the goods and services we need. By adopting a sustainability mind-set when purchasing, our input can drive future market values. Supporting companies that value sustainable manufacturing practices is easy. The research has already been done, and there are plenty of lists of companies

SEEK THE SUSTAINABLE

Today there are lots of sustainable alternatives to consider for furniture and building materials. Here are just a few to look into:

Bamboo: If you like wood flooring, choose a sustainable product like bamboo.

Repurposed wood: Reclaimed from old barns or other sources, this makes great flooring and furniture.

Cork: This fast-growing material is harvested from living trees, making it a great sustainable option for flooring.

Recycled plastic: If you're looking for some outdoor material, companies are starting to create "timber" out of recycled plastic that's used in decking, fencing, and outdoor furniture. It's easy to maintain and can last a lifetime.

Rigid foam from plant-based polyurethane: First developed for surfboards, this rigid foam made from sustainable plants like bamboo and kelp is now available as building insulation.

that use and promote sustainable practices. The same sources that provide lists of green candidates also keep track of businesses that are doing a good job of sustainable manufacturing. There are also plenty of websites whose sole purpose is to track and present information about green businesses and green lifestyles in general. A brief list includes Green Matters, Cozy Earth, and TreeHugger.

Many companies will self-promote their green practices; some of these are legitimate, and some aren't. Beware of greenwashing tactics that some companies use to make themselves seem more environmentally conscious than they are.

✳ ✳ ✳

Actions You Can Take

SEED

Make sure to vote. By researching which candidates have the best environmental policies and giving them your vote, you can help shape the future of your area and your country. This is a direct way to make sure everything from local development to national manufacturing regulations takes a sustainable turn.

SPROUT

Avoid fast fashion in all forms. Buy from manufacturers that use renewable sources and sustainable processes to make their products. Avoid fibers made from plastics or other petroleum products (polyester, acrylic, nylon, etc.). Purchase clothing that utilizes renewable fibers like lyocell or bamboo. Seek out companies that recycle fabric and send used clothing to them.

TREE

Build sustainably. If you're building or renovating your home or any other structure, do your best to use sustainable materials such as bamboo, reclaimed wood, and other recycled products. You can also get involved in local planning to make sure that the land around you is developed in a sustainable way and that the planners are considering the local habitats.

- 4 -

Renewable Energy

The shift to renewable energy sources is happening all around us, but what does that really mean? By becoming more aware of just how much energy you consume and informing yourself about the different options for energy production that are becoming more and more available, you can make better choices for yourself and become a voice to help shape the future of your community.

Energy Consumption

The United States makes up just 5 percent of the world's population—but we consume 25 percent of the world's oil production. As of 2014, nearly *half* of the oil processed in US refineries was imported from foreign countries, and nearly 30 percent of all petroleum products (including plastics) consumed here came from nondomestic sources. There is no such thing as a renewable fossil fuel: Coal, oil, and natural gas all took millions of years to form. The sun will literally go supernova before enough time goes by to create more fossil fuels. It's this heavy dependence on foreign oil, more than anything, that's driving our nation's interest in alternative energy resources.

In the United States, 63 percent of the electricity is still being generated by fossil fuels, despite the fact that we lead the world in the availability of hydroelectric and geothermal energy potential. Entrenched special interests have lobbied *against* the nation's movement toward renewable

DEFINE YOUR TERMS

Renewable: This word is used to define natural resources (especially energy sources) that are not depleted by use. Examples include wind and solar power; some sources state that water is a renewable energy source, but water is depleted with use and is quite scarce in many areas of the world. To a certain extent, water can replenish itself (in the form of precipitation and condensation), but as the world's population grows, we are using our water—particularly our fresh drinkable water—at a much faster rate than it can replenish itself. *No fossil fuels are renewable.*

Nonrenewable resources: Sometimes called finite resources, nonrenewable resources are natural resources that are not replenishable at the rate at which humanity uses them. They are earth minerals and metal ores that we use to make cars or microchips and fossil fuels to power our lives. While they were integral in the advancement of industrialization and powering our modern world, there are many reasons we should reconsider using them, not limited to the harm their extraction and use cause the environment or the fact that one day these resources will simply run out.

energy; as a result, the energy industry is currently the leading source of cancer-causing air pollution and the second-largest source of CO_2 emissions in the United States. Adopting renewable energy technology is inevitable, and we should be doing it much faster than we are.

Renewable energy sources are generated on Earth via global processes; the trick is figuring out *how* to capture that potential energy and turn it into a way to power our machines. It's also important to note that, while renewable energy is more environmentally sound than fossil fuels, each of these renewables *does* have a carbon footprint, which varies depending on the source of the energy and the technology required to capture it.

Here's a breakdown of global carbon emissions by human activity, in percentage of total emissions:

- Electricity and heat (24.9%)
- Industry (14.7%)
- Transportation (14.3%)
- Other fuel combustion (8.6%)
- Fugitive emissions (4%)
- Agriculture (13.8%)
- Land-use change (12.2%)
- Industrial processes (4.3%)
- Waste (3.2%)

To show what a staggering difference there is between renewable and nonrenewable energy production, the chart on the following page compares the size of the average carbon footprints of various energy sources in terms of the carbon dioxide produced per kilowatt-hour (kwh). **Note:** Not every single wind turbine, hydroelectric dam, or coal plant will have the exact same carbon footprint value; the figures cited in the table on the next page are meant for comparison purposes only.

Renewable Energy Sources

It's easy to see how much of a difference switching to renewables can be, so let's take a closer look at the different options.

BIG NUMBERS The carbon footprint of solar power can vary from 14 to 45 g CO_2/kwh, depending on the type of material used to make the solar panels. Thin-film solar cells (made by depositing a thin layer of photovoltaic material directly onto a substrate, and used in making roof shingles, glazing for skylights, and other building materials) have a smaller footprint than the thicker crystalline silicon photovoltaic cells (which are used in over 90 percent of commercial energy production).

ENERGY SOURCES COMPARED

Use this chart see how much of a difference
switching to renewables can make.

ENERGY SOURCE	CARBON FOOTPRINT (G CO_2/KWH)
Renewable	
Hydro/Ocean	7–8
Wind	11
Geothermal	11.3–47
Solar	14–45
Alternative Energy	
Nuclear	12
Biomass	43
Nonrenewable	
Natural gas	465
Coal	980

Solar

In 1953, a group of scientists created the first silicon solar cell capable of generating enough electricity from sunlight to power small electrical devices. Since then, solar batteries and collection devices have become more efficient at converting the sun's energy into electricity. We are now able to power entire communities with solar energy alone.

The switch to solar electricity production is predicted to expand by an astounding 6,500 percent by the year 2050, according to energy watchdog group DNV GL.

Of all the Earth's potential energy sources, none is greater than the power of the sun. While the amount of solar energy that reaches the surface of the Earth can vary due to weather conditions, seasons, and time of day, many of these issues can be overcome with better battery storage and charging methods. As fossil fuels continue to be depleted, solar energy will remain abundant, stable, and reliable; the costs associated with converting solar energy into electricity will continue to go down as we improve the technology and availability of access.

Hydroelectric Power

Water is considered a renewable resource because it isn't consumed in the process of generating power. Whether passing through turbines in a dam, or flowing over a wheel that turns a stone to grind grain or saw lumber, the water flows out at the end of the process relatively unchanged from the state in which it entered. But, whether or not water is *truly* a renewable resource is debatable. Though it's true that water is replenished by precipitation and sometimes by underground aquifers, the fact is that the water cycle on Earth is a closed system—that is, no outside sources are going to replace the water we use up.

Hydroelectric power is currently generated by capturing the kinetic energy in moving water using turbines, which convert the movement into electricity. Oceans can be a source of hydropower by converting the movement of the tides into electricity. Until recently, tidal power was expensive due to the amount of construction required to capture it and the limited number of sites with sufficient tide range or velocity. New technology has solved these problems, and

TAKE THE LEED

The US Green Building Council's LEED (Leadership in Energy and Environmental Design) system is a program used around the world to rate how green a building is. The system gives building owners and those looking to build new structures a framework for creating "healthy, highly efficient, and cost-saving green buildings." To find out more about what makes a building green, you can go to www.usgbc.org/discoverleed. Once you know what it takes, you can advocate in your community, school, and workplace to make existing and new buildings go green.

CONSERVE WHAT YOU CAN

While it's incredibly important to switch to renewable energy, it's also of the utmost importance to conserve energy resources when you can, especially when you can't help but use nonrenewables. Here are some tips for conservation:

Conserve everyday resources.

Turn off lights in empty rooms. Shut off computers when not in use, instead of allowing them to sit in sleep mode (they continue to pull energy if not turned off). Keep appliance doors closed (don't let the refrigerator door stand open, and use the window in the oven to check on food so that heat doesn't escape). Don't let the water run while brushing teeth or washing dishes (dishwashers actually use less water per load than handwashing). Turn down thermostats in winter and raise them in summer. If you're someone who gets cold easily, find a nice, thrifted wool or other natural fiber sweater! Cozy lap blankets or throws are another option. You can save 10 percent per year on heating and cooling costs this way.

Invest in your home.

Make sure your home is well insulated and in good repair. An estimated 10 to 25 percent of our average heating and cooling expenses is leaking out of poorly sealed windows. Seal cracks around windows and exterior doors, add weather stripping, and install exterior or interior storm windows over older single-pane windows or replace the windows with new low-E glass. These measures lower the amount of energy required to heat and cool the home and can save as much as 35 percent of costs annually.

Make well-considered travel choices.

Use public transportation and walk or bike whenever you can to cut down on your environmental impact and decrease emissions. Reconsider all nonessential travel, especially if it involves flying, which is the most heavily polluting form of transportation. Reduce international travel unless absolutely necessary and travel conscientiously. Consider going by train when possible. City tours by bus are a good way to take in the sights, and group travel is much more sustainable than solo.

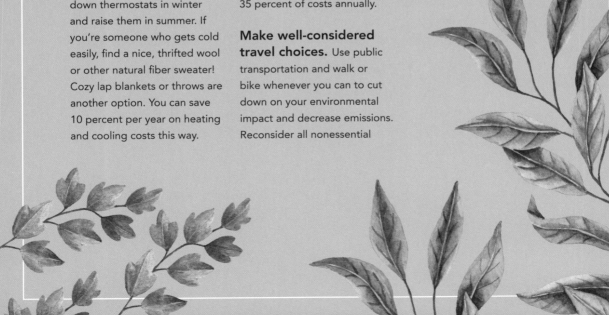

tidal power is poised to become a significant energy source in the near future.

About 40 percent of the renewable electric power generated in the United States in 2018 was hydroelectric. Most hydroelectric power is gathered from dams on high-volume rivers. But damming rivers is fraught with environmental problems, including blocking wildlife (especially fish) migrations, flooding habitats, changing water quality and temperature, and destroying downstream water flows. The last large-scale hydroelectric dam in the United States was the New Melones Dam in California, built in 1979. Because of concerns over environmental impacts, the 1986 Electric Consumers Protection Act requires that non-power values be given equal weight with public power needs when considering power plant licensing requests. It is unlikely that any new major projects like New Melones will be built in the United States.

Smaller projects, like so-called "run-of-the-river" (ROR) plants, have been installed over the years, decreasing some of the undesirable side effects of dam building. These plants allow the river water to flow through the dam without stopping, which keeps sediment from building up behind the dam and prevents deoxygenation and salination of downstream flows.

Because ROR systems don't have big reservoirs, the amount of power generated by the system varies with the flow rate of the river. This can be significant on smaller rivers that may slow down considerably during dry months or when being used for irrigation. This means that RORs tend to be seasonal or intermittent sources of power, which can be tricky for communities.

Wind Power

Wind turbines work much like water turbines: Wind turns the turbine blades, which turn drive trains in generators to

BIG NUMBERS Wind energy emits around 11 g CO_2/kwh, according to a study from the Department of Energy. Coal, meanwhile, emits about 870 g CO_2/kwh and natural gas emits roughly 465 g CO_2/kwh.

create electricity. A gearbox usually regulates the speed of the turn rate. Turbine setups can be horizontal or vertical, though horizontal is much more efficient and more common. Some turbines (especially in historic settings) use wind to turn machinery *directly* rather than converting the power into electricity. This is most common in milling and pumping applications.

The carbon footprint of wind energy is one of the smallest of all energy sources, not just renewables. While it's true that wind power (as with nearly all renewable energy sources) has a life cycle emissions cost as a result of the manufacture of turbine and generator parts, plants, and maintenance, those costs are still considerably lower than the life cycle emissions costs of fossil fuels.

What wind lacks in reliability, it makes up for in lack of emissions and the potential for use in the remotest of areas. What we need is a technology change that improves our ability to capture and store the kinetic energy of wind, and greater ability to predict its flow.

Geothermal

Geothermal refers to the energy from the heat stored in the Earth's crust. Water heated in geothermal hot springs can be used to heat spaces directly (which it's done from Roman times to now) or to generate electricity by drawing steam off of the hot water and using it to power steam turbines. Geothermal heat is collected by drilling deep into the Earth; the deeper you drill, the hotter it gets. But deep drilling is expensive, which is why having the heat close to the surface in natural hot spots is much more cost-effective. Such spots are rare, however.

Advantages of geothermal energy include cost-effectiveness, reliability, sustainability, and environmental friendliness. Historically,

WHAT WIND LOOKS LIKE

One of the concerns of wind energy opponents is the construction of wind farms with their dozens, or even hundreds, of massive turbines. Not only are these extremely unsightly, but they pose a genuine hazard to bird life. A recent statement from the secretary of the Department of the Interior claimed that as many as 750,000 birds a year might be killed by wind turbines. This number was not backed by scientific studies and is therefore debatable. However, the Bureau of Land Management has determined that up to a million birds per year *are* being killed as a result of oil fields, which are also known producers of greenhouse gas emissions, water and air pollution, and groundwater contamination.

however, its use has been limited to areas with naturally occurring hot springs or where heat vents are close to the surface (such as where the Earth's tectonic plates meet and cross). New technologies have greatly increased the distance from such areas that thermal heat can be utilized, and have made its application to smaller, home heating needs possible.

The efficiency of geothermal electric plants is low (10 to 23 percent), because geothermal waters don't get as hot as the steam from boilers, and some of the heat is lost as exhaust. Cost-effectiveness requires producing more electricity than the pumps consume, which can be marginal. However, since geothermal power sources don't vary (unlike wind or water), as much as 96

THE LITTLE THINGS

Conserving energy is a global issue, but there are a lot of little things you can do to save energy at home, work, or school.

- When incandescent lightbulbs die, replace them with LED lightbulbs.

- Turn off the lights when you leave a room.

- Unplug appliances and electronics when not in use, from your microwave to your computer to your phone charger.

- Use curtains as bonus insulation—in the winter, open curtains when it's sunny for some free heat, and close them when the sun goes down to block the chill from coming in and the heat from escaping.

- Open a window instead of running the AC when possible.

- Ride a bike, walk, or take public transportation whenever you can.

percent of the potential energy is actually available for use.

The carbon footprint of geothermal is also quite low, ranging from 11.3 to 47 g CO_2/kwh (depending on the technology used to acquire it). The life cycle emissions cost is considerably less than the costs of fossil fuels due to the sustainability of geothermal energy.

Alternative Energy Sources

Alternative energy sources may or may not be renewable. Some have side effects or potentially toxic concerns that limit the extent to which they are truly renewable. Let's look at some of these.

Nuclear Pros and Problems

At this time, 19 percent of the electricity used in the United States is generated by nuclear power plants. More than 100 nuclear plants were built here in the 1970s and 1980s; most of these are still in operation, though some have become quite dilapidated. Once touted as safe, clean, and never-ending, nuclear power now faces an uncertain future due to a number of issues—not the least of which is nuclear waste disposal. More than 30 percent of the nuclear facilities in the United States are facing closure due to unprofitability or scheduled retirement.

But closing working nuclear facilities is problematic as well, because the electricity produced at productive nuclear sites would most likely be replaced by cheaper electricity from natural gas or coal-fired plants—both of which are much higher in CO_2 emissions than nuclear power. The carbon footprint of nuclear power is about 12 g CO_2/kwh, lower than almost any other energy source, including renewables. But CO_2 isn't the only consideration.

Nuclear power works by splitting atoms of uranium inside a nuclear reactor and harnessing the energy that results to superheat water to over 500°F. The steam from this water is used to drive steam turbines and generate electricity, the same as in fossil fuel power plants.

HUMAN POWERED!

Using your own body's energy to do small chores, like using a manual mower for your lawn or pulling weeds instead of using a weed whacker, not only saves you money on energy consumption but also burns calories to help you stay in shape.

THE PROBLEM OF NUCLEAR WASTE

As promising as harnessing atomic energy can seem, there are serious problems with it.

Uranium is a rare metal, and it is also highly radioactive. It is used in nuclear reactors because it is the "heaviest" natural element, by virtue of having the greatest number of protons in its nucleus. The size of the atom means that the atomic force holding it together is "spread thin," if you will, and the atom can be split apart relatively easily (a process referred to as *fission*). Splitting atoms sets off a chain reaction inside the reactor, which, if left unmodified, would cause a meltdown. Instead, the reaction is controlled using control rods that absorb the excess neutrons from the fission.

Uranium mining is hazardous to the environment. Mining any metal has issues, but uranium has the added problem that *mine tailings* (the materials left over after the uranium is removed from the metal ore) are also radioactive. This material must be forever isolated from contact with the environment. Mine tailings in general are hazardous because they lead to soil erosion, water contamination, and heavy metal runoff into the environment; mine tailings are a worldwide problem.

Since the concentration of uranium in the Earth's crust is low (around 2 parts per million), a lot of waste rock and dirt (called *overburden*) is also generated in order to secure sufficient quantities of uranium. This is a huge disturbance to the land itself, to wildlife habitat, and to potential reclamation efforts.

Disposing of uranium has yet another set of problems. In addition to all of these issues associated with mining uranium, there's the enormous concern of what to do with spent fuel rods. After it's mined, uranium has to be processed for use in a nuclear reactor. This means packing it into long fuel rods to make fuel assemblies that can be used in the core of the reactor. Once all the possible atoms in a rod have been used, the still highly radioactive rod needs to be replaced.

Prior to the Carter administration, these spent fuel rods were planned to be reprocessed into plutonium-based nuclear weapons. President Carter banned nuclear reprocessing using spent fuel cores in 1977, out of fears surrounding nuclear weapons proliferation that might result from civilian uranium fuel access. This ban was lifted by President Reagan in 1981, but commercial uranium reprocessing never resumed.

Faced with disposal of still-radioactive fuel rods, the Department of Energy had to come up with solutions for long-term storage. Nearly $5 billion has already been spent on creating a disposal site at Yucca Mountain in Nevada, despite the fact that no official designation of a government-regulated site has been made and that Nevada residents have opposed the project for the last 30 years. No spent fuel rods have "officially" been sent there.

THERMAL REACTORS

Thermal energy use is common around the world,
but it has its problems.

How They Work

The majority of thermal plants are powered by fossil fuels or nuclear decay; a few use the heat generated by the decomposition or burning of biomass. In addition to powering steam turbines, thermal energy can drive waste incineration plants that convert bulky solid waste into gas, particulates, and heat. This heat can, in turn, be captured and reused again to drive steam turbines, making thermal plants with heat-recovery technology more efficient and profitable.

Why They're a Problem

There's a huge environmental concern with incinerators, however, particularly those built more than 20 years ago. Most older incinerators do not have separators to remove hazardous waste, recyclable materials, and noncombustibles from the waste to be burned. This causes toxic gases to be created and piles of unburnable trash inside the incinerator. It also destroys materials that could have been profitably recycled.

Old Issues

Older incinerators also lack scrubbers to remove toxic gases and particulates from smokestacks before they are released into the atmosphere; as a result, employees and people living near the incinerator can be exposed to dangerously high levels of these substances. There is a large body of evidence supporting the incidence of higher rates of lung disease and various cancers in populations living near polluting incinerators.

Mining uranium, like all mining, is hazardous to the environment, and after it's mined, it undergoes a lot of processing to make it usable in a nuclear reactor. Processed uranium is packed into long fuel rods, which are then bundled together to make fuel assemblies to be used in the core of the reactor. Once that fuel is used up (that is, no more atoms in it can be split), the rods have to be replaced—but they are still extremely radioactive.

Spent fuel (more than 90,000 tons of it) is largely still being stored at the nuclear power plants that created it; the plants were never meant as long-term storage facilities, and the waste-holding capacity is filling fast. Just transporting the radioactive rods offsite is a dangerous undertaking, never mind providing secure and (relatively) safe long-term storage. And we're talking really long term. The time it takes for radioactive material to lose *half* of its radioactivity is termed the *half-life*. The radioactive half-life of the U-235 isotope used in nuclear reactors is 704 million years.

This concern sums up why nuclear energy can't really be considered a renewable power source: It's far too dangerous to the Earth and all of its living inhabitants.

Biomass

Biomass refers to organic materials such as agriculture and forest residues, energy crops, and algae that are used to generate energy. Basically, it can come from any biological material derived from living or recently living

BIG NUMBERS The carbon emissions from natural gas usage are nearly 40 times greater (465 g CO_2/kwh versus 12 g CO_2/kwh) than nuclear power. The United States is number two on the list of the top five CO_2-emitting countries in the world. We can't afford to become number one.

organisms that stores sunlight as chemical energy. While the Earth has a biomass of living animals, plants, and humans, biomass as it refers to energy production is mainly concerned with plant materials.

The renewable energy produced from biomass (aka bioenergy) familiar to most of us is biodiesel, which is made from corn, soybeans, and a few other crops. Biofuels like this are playing an important role as short-term substitutes for gasoline. In 2015, production of 14.7 billion gallons of ethanol, another kind of biofuel, meant that the United States was able to import 527 million fewer barrels of crude oil to produce gasoline. In that year, the ethanol industry contributed an estimated $4.8 billion in tax revenue to the Department of the Treasury. And that ethanol was all produced domestically.

It's not just the combustion of biowaste that can produce fuel. Off-gassing, which occurs when organic materials break down under oxygen-poor conditions, can also be collected and used in much the same way as natural gas.

The Department of Energy website states: "When managed well, biomass resources can also provide important land, habitat, and soil benefits. For example, some plants grown for bioenergy (like native prairie grasses) can be grown on soils that have poor fertility and cannot be used for farming. They also have the potential to improve soil health, provide habitats for wildlife, and help prevent pollution from entering nearby waterways."

The merits of this statement are debatable: Though it's true that native

BIG POSSIBILITIES

The *2016 Billion-Ton Report: Advancing Domestic Resources for a Thriving Bioeconomy*, produced by the US Department of Energy, concluded that the United States has the potential to produce 1 billion dry tons of nonfood biomass resources annually by 2040 and still meet demands for food, feed, and fiber. One billion tons of biomass could

- produce up to 50 billion gallons of biofuels,

- yield 50 billion pounds of bio-based chemicals and bioproducts (maybe not so great?),

- generate 85 billion kwh of electricity (enough to power 7 million homes), and

- contribute 1.1 million jobs and $259 billion in revenue to the economy.

AN ABUNDANCE OF BIOMASS

There's a growing problem of invasion of ecosystems by nonnative organisms, and they're full of potential fuel.

Natives vs. Nonnatives

Native plants have adapted to the specific growing conditions in every biome, and wildlife have come to depend on the food resources those plants provide.

Nonnatives are frequently able to outcompete natives (both plants and animals) for resources and tend to push natives out of the ecosystem altogether. Unfortunately, this has a lot of unforeseen side effects, including the starvation and subsequent extinction of native species, as well as alteration of the landscape.

A Fiery Issue

A recent study conducted by researchers in Australia showed that the increasing numbers of invasive nonnative grasses in the ecosystem were a hazard not just because they displace native species that wildlife depend on, but also because many of them are much more flammable and conducive to creating large fires than are natives. The study was published in November 2019—at the same time, catastrophic bush fires destroyed 50 million acres of land and killed more than 1.25 billion animals in Australia. Smoke from those fires could be detected as far away as Chile and Argentina.

While there were a number of factors contributing to the enormity of the 2019 bush fires (including drought, record heat, and sustained winds), the fuel load served up by invasive nonnative grasses was notable.

Algae Invasion

Algae (a broad range of organisms that live in water and use chlorophyll) are another source of problems and potential solutions. They are becoming a worldwide problem due to fertilizer runoff from farming operations. They clog rivers and streams on land, and can create "dead zones" in oceans by using all of the available oxygen in the water. "Algal blooms" are common contributors to such dead zones.

In addition to wild algae, many strains are being developed in laboratories for a diverse number of applications. Some can grow in industrial wastewater, sparing clean water resources while providing bioenergy; others are being developed to consume crude oil to potentially clean up environmental oil spills.

BIOMASS SOURCES

Biomass comes from many different plants and places, some of which may surprise you:

- Crop wastes
- Forest residues
- Purpose-grown grasses
- Woody energy crops
- Microalgae
- Industrial waste
- Wood processing waste
- Urban wood waste (construction)
- Urban landscape waste
- Food waste
- Livestock and animal waste
- Soiled animal bedding
- Municipal waste (combustible)
- Treated sewer sludge

plants (particularly grasses) are better able to grow on poor soils than agricultural crops are, and that native plants provide wildlife habitat and prevent soil erosion, harvesting those plants for biofuel is going to completely negate those same benefits. Harvest machinery damages thin, fragile soils—particularly soils on poor sites. Harvesting the plants also means that animals have nothing to eat and nowhere to live. Native plants take *years* to grow large enough to provide the food resources that wildlife depends on, making them ill-suited for sustainable harvest by humans.

Renewable but Not Sustainable

So, why is biomass not a viable renewable energy source? The problem is long-term sustainability. As the human population grows, we'll need more land to feed ourselves

and to support urban areas for us to live in. We'll have progressively less and less "empty" land to devote to the production of nonfood crops. So, growing corn to make ethanol fuel won't make sense because the crop uses a lot of land and a lot of water

BIG NUMBERS The United States is already committing some 40 percent of the corn we grow to the production of biofuel. Approximately 17 billion gallons of ethanol fuel was produced in the United States in 2019, representing less than 12 percent of an estimated 143 billion gallons of total gasoline consumed that year. In other words, even if we doubled the percentage of corn we grow for biofuel, we would still only be able to provide less than 25 percent of the gasoline we use.

SUSTAINABLE PLANTS FOR BIOMASS

Bamboo is an example of a grass that can be sustainably harvested for a number of purposes, including to produce biomass for energy production. Other examples of sustainable, nonfood bioenergy crops include sweet sorghum, wheatgrass, miscanthus, tall fescue, and fast-growing hardwoods like silver maple, cottonwood, hybrid willows, and poplars. Green ash is on this list, but in recent years this species has suffered intense predation by emerald ash borers, which kill the trees. Black walnut is also a fast-growing tree, but it produces a highly desirable nut crop and a valuable furniture wood; using it for biofuel would be a waste of its resources.

(which is already running dangerously low in many areas of the world).

One acre of soybeans produces roughly 50 to 55 gallons of biodiesel—enough to fill an average SUV about three times. Keep in mind, however, that it takes an entire growing season to produce that 50 gallons, and it gets burned up in less than a month by *one* car. This is why biofuels are not sustainable in the long run. They do, however, have a place as a cleaner interim energy source while we create the new technology needed to convert the world from fossil fuels to truly renewable sustainable energy.

Nonfood-based biofuels—such as those made from grasses or farm waste—offer huge potential for cutting fossil fuel use and carbon emissions. The best cellulose-based ethanol (i.e., that made from the nonedible parts of plants) can produce 90 percent fewer global warming emissions compared to gasoline, according to the Union of Concerned Scientists.

Vegetative composting and combustion are ancient practices that still have merit in today's world. Though burning vegetation releases carbon into the atmosphere, the amounts are smaller than what's released through burning fossil fuels. Biopower from burning organic materials has a carbon footprint of about 43 g CO_2/kwh, versus the 980 g CO_2/kwh of coal and 465 of natural gas. So please don't believe propaganda that tries to convince us that natural gas is a "clean" energy source. Burning wood is literally 10 times cleaner than natural gas, and 23 times cleaner than coal.

* * *

Actions You Can Take

SEED

Go "small solar." Take advantage of small tools that use alternative energy resources. Examples include solar-powered lawn mowers, leaf blowers, and trimmers, and solar USB chargers. There are even solar-powered fountains for the backyard!

SPROUT

Choose renewable for yourself. If you own your residence, you could instead choose to convert your home to solar power. In many states, there are tax advantages or stipends for making this switch. Solar panels have improved tremendously in the last decade and are lighter weight and more efficient than ever.

TREE

Go "off-grid." Depending on your locality, you may be able to disconnect from the community power grid and make use of alternative energy sources such as wind or hydroelectric. Unhooking from municipal utilities is not easy, unless you have some land you can build on. In addition to home heating needs, generating your own electricity via solar battery chargers, wind turbines, or even water mills might be possible. Cooking in wood-fired or charcoal stoves and utilizing a septic tank instead of municipal sewage treatment are some other ideas worth exploring.

- 5 -

A Clean Home

It's no secret that our world is awash in a sea of chemicals. More than 80,000 chemicals are used to produce the many common household products we use in the United States. From medicines to insecticides, cosmetics to house paints, it's impossible to completely escape chemicals—and we really wouldn't want to. Thousands of beneficial chemicals help keep food from spoiling, create cures for diseases, and keep our bodies functioning their best. But there are also a lot of chemicals that are harmful—some accidentally, some intentionally—that we need to avoid. Let's look at some of the problematic household chemicals and then how to replace them with green alternatives.

Indoor Pollution

According to the Centers for Disease Control and Prevention, the air in our homes and buildings is usually more polluted than the outside air—even in major cities. The following page has a short list of some of the more harmful chemicals commonly found in our homes.

Nearly all of our food is contaminated by chemicals, from steroids and antibiotics in animal products, to pesticide, animal waste, and particulate residues on produce. Prepared and packaged foods contain preservatives as well as artificial colors and flavors. Dairy products have emulsifiers, preservatives, and thickening agents—some natural like tapioca, some not. (See the next chapter for a list of fruits and vegetables with the highest amounts of pesticide residues.)

Indoor Air Pollution

Air pollution was one of the first concerns of environmentalists at the beginning of the conservation movement, due to smog from industrial manufacturing. The Environmental Protection Agency (EPA) was created in 1970 in the wake of public pressure to address environmental hazards and protect human health. It does *not* have purview over wildlife, wetlands, nuclear waste, or food safety.

We spend most of our time indoors, but indoor air is often more polluted than outdoor air: Smoke, pet dander, dust, air fresheners, paint fumes (VOCs), household cleaners, mold, mildew, and potentially billions of microorganisms are some of the possible contaminants. The EPA has ranked indoor air quality as one of the top five environmental risks to public health. Studies have found that indoor air pollutants are typically two to five times greater (and in some cases 100 times greater) than outdoor pollution levels. Reasons include having poor ventilation, burning toxic candles, and using air fresheners and chemical-laden household cleaners.

Because our bodies use oxygen to neutralize and remove toxins, the air we breathe needs to be oxygen-rich. Air is low in oxygen content when it is polluted, which means less oxygen and more toxins entering the bloodstream.

WATER POLLUTION

Using a good-quality water filter on home faucets (including showerheads) is an effective step toward decreasing exposure to chemical toxins. Brita and Pür are two manufacturers of good-quality filters.

INDOOR AIR POLLUTANTS

We often don't think of the air inside as subject to pollution, but there are a number of household chemicals that can degrade your air quality.

CHEMICAL	FOUND IN	DAMAGE CAUSED
Formaldehyde	Air fresheners, nail polish	Nerve damage
Ammonia	Kitchen and window cleaners	Respiratory irritant
Sodium hydroxide (lye)	Oven and drain cleaners	Caustic irritant
Hydrochloric acid	Toilet bowl cleaners	Tissue damage
Chlorine bleach	Laundry and dishwasher detergents	Lung damage
Perchloroethylene	Carpet cleaners	Carcinogen
VOCs (volatile organic compounds)	Paint, new furniture, new car "smell"	Irritant; carcinogen
Polytetrafluoroethylene/ Teflon	Nonstick coatings on cookware	Carcinogen
Naphthalene	Mothballs	Destroys red blood cells
Nitrobenzene	Furniture polish	Carcinogen
Carbon monoxide	Space heaters, camp stoves	Respiratory failure
Triclosan and triclocarban	Antibacterial soaps	Create antibiotic-resistant bacteria
Lead (element, not a chemical)	Pre-1970s paint, lead plumbing	Poisonous to children
Flame-retardant chemicals	Clothing, upholstery, mattresses	Birth defects

The EPA is also responsible for many concerns relating to the energy use and greenhouse gas emissions of home appliances. To help us make the best purchasing decisions, the EPA oversees the manufacture of certain consumer goods. Programs administered by the EPA include Energy Star (relating to appliance energy efficiency), Smart Growth (which supports development of sustainable communities), WaterSense (which encourages efficient water-use mechanisms), and Safer Choice (which labels products for chemical safety).

Why Air Quality Matters

Since the early 1980s, the occurrence of asthma has been rising across all races, classes, and age groups. Asthma has become a silent epidemic with disastrous effects on our quality of life. In 1999, about 20 million Americans suffered from asthma—about 1 in every 14 people. Current estimates put the number at around 1 in 12. Worldwide estimates indicate that some 340 million people suffer from asthma.

Fine or ultra-fine particulate matter is easily inhaled and can pass into the bloodstream, and even cross the blood–brain barrier. Dry eyes, headaches, nasal congestion, fatigue, and nausea are common symptoms of respiratory contamination; serious conditions such as asthma, lung infections, and lung cancer also occur. Particulates in the bloodstream have been linked to stroke and depression in adults, while children have

IMPROVING INDOOR AIR QUALITY

Here are some simple things you can do to help make the air in your home better to breathe:

- Eliminate sources of air contaminants: paints, adhesives, polishes, etc.

- Avoid harsh chemical air fresheners and cleaning products.

- Keep mold and mildew at bay by cleaning up any existing spots and keeping things dry.

- Add a couple of houseplants to your windowsills to act as natural air cleaners. Indoor plants naturally filter and purify air in your home. Easy-to-grow houseplants that can help improve indoor air quality include spider plant, peace lily, pothos (also called devil's ivy), philodendron, lady palm, dieffenbachia, and snake plant. Make sure that you don't overwater houseplants; overwatering can cause the roots to get moldy.

shown increases in systemic inflammation, immune dysfunction, and neural distress.

While outdoor air is generally cleaner than indoor air, people with asthma and allergies suffer from exposure to pollens and spores from outside. Consider HEPA-level window filters to help minimize outdoor particulates. HEPA filters are also available for home heating and cooling systems, which not only pull air from the outside but also move it throughout the house. You'll be amazed at the difference these filters can make to your loved ones suffering from asthma.

Homemade Cleaning Products

Chemicals are ubiquitous in our world, but there are ways to limit your exposure to the most toxic of them—especially at home. Begin by eliminating cleaners that use toxic ingredients and seeking out safer alternatives. Brands such as ECOS, Better Life, Seventh Generation, and Mrs. Meyer's make effective, safer alternatives to chemical cleaning products.

Alternatively, you can try making your own! What follows are recipes that use

SAFETY FIRST

When making your own cleaning compounds at home, be sure to observe a couple of important safety tips. Keep these things in mind no matter which cleaner you're making.

- Clearly label homemade cleaning supplies.

- Mix no more than a month's worth at a time, and store in tightly covered jars or bottles.

- Do not reuse containers from commercial cleaning supplies, as they may contain chemical residues.

- Use glass (ideally) or metal containers to store mixtures; plastic may interact with the mixture and break down or cause off-gassing.

ingredients that are cheap, easy to find, and effective at cleaning everyday messes. You can add essential oils such as lavender, tea tree, citrus, or rosemary for fresh scents and antiseptic benefits.

When using natural ingredients, be aware that they generally take a little bit longer to work than their chemical counterparts, so allow a few minutes for them to sit on the stain. Be sure to scrub gently to avoid scratching surfaces, then rinse well and wipe dry if desired.

continued

TOP TOXINS FOUND IN INDOOR AIR

Without fresh air circulating throughout indoor premises, toxins can build up in our homes, workplaces, and wherever else we gather indoors. Below are some of the most harmful indoor air toxins to try to avoid for healthier lungs in your day-to-day life. For some, there are steps you can take to limit them in your home.

Tobacco Smoke

Smoking has been linked to lung cancer for decades. It's also been linked to the risk for many other cancers, including breast and colorectal cancer. In addition to various cancers, there is high risk to the still-developing organs and brains of children.

Quitting smoking is not easy, but the benefits of quitting far outweigh the difficulty. Studies have shown that within two weeks of quitting smoking, our lung tissues begin to heal. Depending on how long you've smoked, you can potentially regain full function of your lungs. When we stop smoking, our skin becomes less rough and our eyes quit tearing. Quitting also benefits those who come in contact with secondhand smoke, including our children and pets.

Paint Fumes

Some paints still on the market give off fumes called volatile organic compounds (VOCs). Though they tend to dissipate fairly quickly, inhalation of VOCs is still hazardous. Over time, the buildup of these compounds can lead to headaches, loss of coordination, liver damage, and other issues. Many paints come with warning labels stating they should be used only in well-ventilated areas.

All major paint manufacturers offer low-VOC interior paints. Some even offer "ultra-low-VOC" paints specifically designed for baby rooms. Low-VOC carpeting and adhesives are also available for purchase.

Microorganisms

Biological contaminants include living organisms or their derivatives, bacteria, dust mites, household dust (which is largely made up of human skin cells and dead mites), and viruses. These contaminants build up in the body to toxic levels and can cause respiratory illnesses, allergies, and sleep disorders, among other things. Children, the elderly, and people with weakened immune systems are particularly susceptible to airborne biological contaminants.

Clean the air using air filters—HEPA filters and Guardian Air REME are excellent options. Filters are available for home heating and AC units, or as freestanding machines for individual rooms.

Pet Dander

Pet dander (particles of fur and skin) can be inhaled or swallowed, causing respiratory distress. An estimated 30 percent of allergy sufferers are pet owners. Frequent vacuuming using a vacuum fitted with a HEPA filter can help improve symptoms.

Dust with a damp cloth or electrostatically charged duster to remove particulate matter. Heavy dust collections may need HEPA-filtered vacuuming. Don't just spread the dust around with regular dusting.

Mold and Mildew

Mold occurs naturally in the environment. Mold spores enter

the home through open doors and windows, and on shoes and clothing. Once inside, the spores can multiply dramatically and become an inhalation hazard.

Mold is typically green or black and grows underneath wet surfaces. It is usually fuzzy or slimy. Mildew, on the other hand, is usually white, yellow, or gray and is found in warm, moist areas like bathrooms; it is typically powdery or fluffy.

Improving ventilation goes a long way toward decreasing mold and mildew. Cleaner, drier outside air—or even air that is circulated by a fan—helps dehumidify the area and discourage the moisture that mold and mildew love. Ventilation also keeps the concentration of air pollutants from building up inside your home. Be wary when cleaning up mold or mildew; scrubbing makes the spores become airborne and you can inhale them while cleaning. Serious infestations of mold should be handled by professionals specializing in such cleanups.

Furniture Danger

Flame retardants such as polybrominated diphenyl ethers (PBDEs) and chlorinated tris (TDCPP) are widely used in the polyurethane foam stuffing of furniture, automobile interiors, and carpet padding. They are also present in children's products, such as toys, strollers, car seats, nursing pillows, and sleeping mats.

TDCPP is a known carcinogen. Newer flame-retardant chemicals appear to have the same hazards. Inhalation is the primary route of exposure. Do your best to buy products that are proud to promote they are free of these chemicals.

Candles

Candles are lovely and make nice gifts, but the type of candle you buy and burn matters. Most candles, especially scented ones made with paraffin wax, emit benzene and toluene, two known carcinogens. Paraffin wax candles also emit hydrocarbons called alkanes and alkenes, *two of the chemicals found in car exhaust!*

If you want to purchase candles, choose soy- or beeswax-based varieties scented only with pure essential oils.

Glymes

Glymes are a class of chemical solvents, particularly dimethoxyethane, that can be found in brake fluid, paints, lithium batteries, inkjet cartridges, and carpet cleaners. These industrial chemicals have been linked to developmental and reproductive damage. In 2011, the EPA announced new measures regarding the use of glymes in consumer products, which included requirements that the manufacturer notify the agency of the use of glymes and subsequent review of the product's safety. To decrease potential exposure to glymes, make sure the area is well ventilated when you're painting, use natural carpet cleaners, and consider having your photos printed at the store rather than printing them at home.

Wood Smoke

Research has shown that regular inhalation of wood smoke suppresses immune activity, much like exposure to cigarette smoke does. In addition to particulates, smoke contains benzenes, dioxins, aldehydes, hydrocarbons, carbon dioxide, and high levels of deadly carbon monoxide. It may also contain heat-resistant mold spores and many other substances.

Anyone who burns wood indoors needs to be aware of potential health risks. Many of the chemicals in wood smoke remain concentrated in the ash and dust long after the fire is extinguished. Wear a mask and avoid stirring up the ash as much as possible when cleaning out your home's fireplace. Dispose of ash outdoors in sealed bags. Or you could use the wood ash in your garden's compost pile. Ash by itself can be caustic, so it's best to compost this material rather than using it directly in the garden.

While white vinegar is sometimes too acidic for certain surfaces—like granite, marble, stone, hardwood floors, and cast-iron pans—it is generally effective at cleaning windows, mirrors, glass, drains, garbage disposals, bathroom steel fixtures that suffer from mineral deposits, hard water buildup, soap scum, laminate, ceramic tile, ovens, refrigerators, microwaves, dishwashers, and stainless steel.

The following recipes for DIY cleaning products are organized by the starring ingredient. You'll be surprised how much you can get done without chemicals!

White Vinegar

White vinegar is a mild acid used for everything from salad dressings to hair rinses. Pickling foods uses the acidity of vinegar and the alkalinity of salt to preserve meats and vegetables because the acidity kills bacteria and mold spores. Vinegar is also effective at breaking the chemical bonds that keep organic smells (like pet urine) locked in fabrics. Research has found that the bactericidal activity of vinegar *increases* as the temperature of its solution increases, so warming up vinegar-based cleaning solutions can make them more effective.

AMAZING ALL-PURPOSE CLEANER

- 2 tablespoons distilled white vinegar
- 1 teaspoon liquid castile soap (vegetable-based and natural, such as Dr. Bronner's)
- 2 tablespoons baking soda
- 2 cups warm water

Add vinegar and liquid castile soap to a spray bottle and shake gently. Then add the baking soda. When it stops foaming, add the warm water, then shake gently again. Use on counters and kitchen and bathroom surfaces, wiping with a clean cloth.

COPPER AND BRASS CLEANER

- 2 tablespoons flour
- 2 tablespoons white vinegar
- 2 tablespoons iodized table salt

Mix the ingredients in a small glass dish. Rub the paste onto uncoated copper or brass and let it dry (do not use on metals that have a tarnish-free finish; the salt will scratch the finish). Buff off with a lint-free cloth.

VINEGAR SPRAY GLASS AND SURFACE CLEANER

1 cup white vinegar

1 gallon water

Mix the ingredients in a bucket or spray bottle. Spray the mixture on windows, mirrors, toilets, and floors. Use crumpled newspaper to wipe solution off of glass windows and mirrors to leave a lint-free, streak-free shine while also finding another use for newspapers. Recycle or compost newspaper when finished (vinegar-soaked newspaper is safe for composting, unlike papers that are used with chemical sprays).

CITRUS CLEANING SPRAY

Both vinegar and citrus peels contain the acidity and grease-cutting capabilities that make for an unstoppable cleaning force. Together they can dissolve soap scum and other yucky buildups. Add citrus peels to a jar (these can be lemon, orange, grapefruit, or a mix of peels). Fill the jar to the top with white vinegar. Let the mixture sit for two weeks before straining out the peels and diluting 1:1 with water.

SALAD DE-WILTER

This one's pretty cool; white vinegar actually has the ability to perk up wilting leafy greens. If you have some lettuce in the fridge that seems on the verge of going bad, toss the leaves in a mixture of cold water and white vinegar. It will liven up the greens a bit, giving them a few extra days of use. The vinegar increases the acidity of the cells in the leafy greens, resulting in an increase of water absorption in the leaves. You might want to cut off any far-gone, browned parts of the lettuce before bathing it in the water–vinegar mixture.

APPLE CIDER VINEGAR TO DEFROST YOUR CAR

The acidity of vinegar makes ice melt more quickly, but sometimes it's best to use vinegar as a preventive measure on car windows. Spray a mixture of apple cider vinegar and water on your car windows the night before snow or freezing temperatures are expected. The acidity prevents the ice from forming in the first place. Avoid getting the spray solution on the vehicle's paint.

DISHWASHING SOLUTION

Vinegar naturally cuts through grease in a way that not even dish soap always can. To wash dishes, you can use either white or apple cider vinegar. Both have the same grease-cutting effect.

Add 3 to 4 teaspoons of vinegar to your normal dish detergent for best results. For glassware, use a ratio of 1 part vinegar to 3 parts water; let the glassware air-dry. For particularly greasy pans, boil 2 to 3 cups of vinegar directly in the pan; it will restore the pan's original nonstick quality.

These directions are for handwashing; to adapt this to a dishwasher, add the vinegar to the bottom of the machine (increasing the amount to ¼ cup). Always use the air-dry cycle on the dishwasher to save electricity.

LAUNDRY ADDITIVE

Vinegar acts as a triple threat when it's used in laundry: Not only is it a powerful deodorizer, but it also functions as a gentle and nontoxic fabric softener and is exceptional at whitening and brightening your clothes. It's particularly good at removing yellow underarm stains (and odor) from perspiration. To use as a deodorizer, pour ½ cup of distilled white vinegar into the machine in place of conventional detergent. To use vinegar as a fabric softener, pour 1 cup of vinegar into the washing machine during the final rinse cycle.

STAIN PRETREATMENT

Dilute ½ cup of white vinegar in 1 gallon of water and apply the mixture directly to the stain with a clean cloth. Wash as usual. When added to baking soda to make a paste, vinegar can also dissolve red wine, grass, and other organic-based stains. (Before using this stain pretreatment, test for colorfastness using a cotton swab dipped in vinegar.)

CLEAN UP AFTER PETS

Vinegar is handy for deodorizing and removing cat or dog urine stains from carpets. For these purposes, spray the area thoroughly with a white vinegar and water mixture. Allow to soak for an hour, then press with a clean cloth to remove residue. Do not rub the stain; it will only spread the stain and make it bigger, as well as activate the smell.

CAT KEEPER-OFFER

Cats loathe the smell of vinegar, so vinegar spray can be highly effective in dissuading cats from clawing or climbing on furniture. Spray a white vinegar and water mixture on upholstery or on a cloth and leave it on the countertop. Vinegar can be especially effective for cats who "mark their territory" in places other than a litter box. Cat urine is much more concentrated than dog urine, so spray the marked area with undiluted vinegar to eliminate the smell and prevent future incidents.

A WORD OF WARNING

DO NOT spray the cat with vinegar! Vinegar is highly acidic and very damaging to eyes and mucous membranes; it could cause permanent blindness in your cat.

WATER STAINS AND WOOD

For those frustrating times when you or a guest forgets to use a coaster, vinegar can help. It actually rids wooden furniture of that annoying water ring. All you have to do is take a mixture of equal parts white vinegar and vegetable oil and rub it on the stained surface, going with the grain. When the ring is gone, wipe off the oily residue with a clean, dry cloth.

KEEP FLOWERS FRESH

Vinegar helps keep flowers looking fresh in the vase. It acts as a natural preservative by killing microorganisms in the water and helps the cut flowers take up water through their stems. Dissolve 3 tablespoons of sugar and 2 tablespoons of apple cider vinegar per quart of warm water. The stems should be covered with 3 to 4 inches of the mixture for optimal results. To keep the bouquet looking its best, remove submerged leaves from the stems.

GOO GONE ALTERNATIVE

Who needs Goo Gone or Krud Kutter when you have a gallon of household vinegar at your disposal? The acetic acid in vinegar is strong enough to cut through the sticky mess that things like bumper stickers, labels, and tape leave behind.

Saturate a paper towel in white vinegar, then place the towel over the adhesive for up to five minutes. Pull up one corner of the sticker—no razor blade required. Instead, you could use a spatula or even a credit card to peel it back. Leftover adhesive residue? Take a clean cloth saturated in white vinegar and rub the affected area. Do not apply the mixture to porous surfaces.

Hydrogen Peroxide

Hydrogen peroxide is a highly reactive oxidizer; it bubbles and fizzes (without smoke) while undergoing chemical reactions. It is a mild antiseptic (at about a 3 percent concentration) and is also the bleaching agent in hair coloring (at a 6 to 10 percent concentration). Fill a spray bottle with a hydrogen peroxide and water mixture and use as you would spray bleach.

A WORD OF WARNING

Although hydrogen peroxide was once commonly used to clean skin wounds, today many doctors don't recommend it because it damages healthy tissue at the same time it's killing bacteria. It's also very corrosive to eyes and mucous membranes.

LAUNDRY STAIN REMOVER AND "OXY" BOOST

Keep hydrogen peroxide near the laundry area because it can be a great spot cleaner on clothing. Test first to ensure it won't fade color on the clothing by dipping a cotton swab into hydrogen peroxide and touching the swab to a hidden area of the fabric. If color transfers to the swab, don't use the solution on that material.

Mix 1 part dishwashing liquid with 2 parts hydrogen peroxide in a spray bottle (don't fill to the top, leave about a third of empty space). Spray the stain thoroughly and let it sit for about an hour. Wash as usual. This is especially effective on yellow stains at collars and armpits, though set-in stains may require scrubbing with baking soda.

To use as an oxy booster, pour 1 cup of straight hydrogen peroxide into the wash water after the machine has filled (to avoid bleaching dark colors). This disinfects and removes odors from clothes.

DISHWASHER CLEANER BOMBS

¼ cup hydrogen peroxide

1–2 cups baking soda

Few drops essential oil of choice (citrus or mint works well)

1 cup white vinegar

2 tablespoons dishwashing liquid

Combine the hydrogen peroxide, baking soda, and essential oil of choice in a glass container. Mix gently until the mixture forms a ball (add or subtract baking soda as needed). Press the mixture into individual ice cube molds, or place small scoops onto aluminum foil. Allow to dry overnight.

Place two or three bombs on the bottom of the dishwasher. Fill a small cup or glass bowl with white vinegar and dishwashing liquid and place it in the top rack of the dishwasher. Run the short wash cycle; allow to air-dry.

GROUT WHITENER

Pour hydrogen peroxide directly onto badly soiled grout, or make a paste with baking soda, and scrub. Heavily soiled grout may need to soak for an hour or so. Rinse well when finished.

CREATING YOUR BEST HOME

When it comes to creating our best home environments, many of us are taking inspiration from around the world.

The Danes have the word *hygge* (HOO guh), which describes a concept that is all about creating a sense of coziness and general well-being. Natural fibers, soft neutral colors, and snuggly warmth are hallmarks of this style.

Others are embracing minimalism, paring down possessions to the essentials that "spark joy," as described by Japanese writer Marie Kondo. Her best-selling book was so popular that charities received record levels of donations of goods in 2018 and 2019. Here are some tips for creating your best—and most natural—home.

Minimize Clutter

Whether you live in a mansion or a tent, there are many benefits to an organized, clutter-free home. You'll save time searching for your necessities like your phone and keys, and you'll save money by not buying duplicates of items that you can't find. And a cluttered home can even cause anxiety or depression in many of us.

Start with the most-used areas of your space, such as the kitchen, living room, and bedrooms. The bedroom may be the first thing to tackle because it's where we go to rest, and if it's a cluttered mess, it can prey on our subconscious mind and affect the quality of our sleep. Get rid of anything you haven't used in the past year—chances are you won't even miss it.

Tackle the closet with a nonjudgmental friend. Have that person hold up each piece of clothing for you to look at but not touch. This part is important because touching things sends a signal of "possession" to the brain, and we are much less likely to be willing to part with things when we touch them. Donate clothes that don't fit, are out of style, or are unflattering—but only donate clothes that are in good condition and stain-free.

Consider getting rid of anything that doesn't make you feel happy, even if it was a gift. You can honor the spirit

behind the gift (and the giver) without keeping the object. Take a picture of the gift, if you want, then create a display or keepsake that includes such pictures. You'll have a space filled with joy instead of junk you don't use.

Employ Nature's Healing Powers

Let the sun shine in! Open the windows regularly to refresh the air in your home. Natural materials support health and wellness in our lives. Choose pillows, rugs, towels, and clothing made from minimally processed natural fibers, such as wool, silk, bamboo, and linen. Stock your kitchen with glass and ceramic dishes and containers instead of plastics. Do the same with furniture choices, seeking out timeless styles made from wood and natural fabrics. Minimally processed natural materials won't off-gas harmful VOCs.

Choose alternative fiber or silk sheets and a wool mattress (or mattress topper) to draw heat and moisture away from your body. A bed dressed with natural fibers will keep you cooler than foam (which holds in heat); plus, foam is made with petroleum-based products, so it releases numerous toxins and volatile compounds—particularly those from fire retardants.

Live plants are an essential part of a natural home environment. Living houseplants remove CO_2 and toxins from indoor air (see page 84 for a list), and seeing green plants can make you feel calmer and happier. Aromatic herbs such as oregano, mint, and sage are also easily grown indoors in pots, and having fresh herbs handy for cooking is an added bonus.

Set a Serene Scene

The modern world is often overstimulating. Try creating a space in your home that is calming—a place that you can go to unwind, de-stress, meditate, or enjoy a quiet cup of tea. Maybe this space is just a comfy chair in one corner of the room or maybe you can devote an entire room to creating a serene getaway within your home. No matter how big or small it is, it's best to use neutral, soft colors and declutter the space as much as possible. A diffuser for organic essential oils or a clean-burning soy candle can help enhance the peacefulness of the space and make it feel special.

———————————

Healthy practices are cumulative: Once you start clearing out the clutter, bringing in nature, and taking time to decompress, you'll notice that you're feeling calmer at home and everywhere else.

FUNGICIDE FOR MOLD AND MILDEW

Hydrogen peroxide is a good fungicide, particularly on items that touch the skin. Spray full-strength hydrogen peroxide on bathroom fixtures, on shower curtains and walls, and beneath shampoo and bodywash bottles that stand in the shower (a perfect spot for slime to form!). Add 2 or 3 tablespoons to small humidifiers or dehumidifiers, up to ½ cup for larger units.

FUNGICIDE FOR HOUSEPLANTS

Make a mixture of ¼ cup of hydrogen peroxide to 1 quart of water. Use it to water houseplants, about once a month in place of regular water. The hydrogen peroxide kills fungus in the soil of potted plants (particularly a problem when houseplants are overwatered) and helps oxygenate the root area. Killing soil fungus also gets rid of those annoying fungus gnats that live in plant pots. Do not make the solution stronger, as it might burn the roots and kill the plant.

Baking Soda

Baking soda absorbs odors and also acts as a mild abrasive. Use it on bathroom and kitchen surfaces to remove stains or to clean inside a messy oven. Adding salt can provide a boost in scrubbing power.

BAKING SODA BATHROOM SCRUB

1 cup baking soda

¼ cup liquid castile soap (vegetable-based and natural, such as Dr. Bronner's)

2 tablespoons vegetable glycerin

5–6 drops tea tree essential oil

In a glass bowl, mix the baking soda and liquid castile soap. Add the vegetable glycerin and tea tree oil. (Glycerin is a natural preservative; tea tree oil has antibacterial properties.) Scrub sinks and other bathroom surfaces with a clean cloth or scrub brush. Rinse with hot water and polish with a dry cloth.

BAKING SODA SURFACE AND CLOTH STAIN REMOVER

Sprinkle baking soda directly on the stain and mix with a few drops of water to make a paste; alternatively, combine ¼ cup of baking soda in a small bowl with enough water to make a paste and then spread on the stain. Allow to sit for a few minutes (don't allow it to dry out), then scrub gently until the stain is gone; wipe with a damp cloth (or launder) until the residue is gone.

Lemon Juice

Lemon juice is an effective bleaching agent and grease cutter that has dozens of uses. (We listed only a couple of favorites here, but you can find many more online.) Lemon juice also kills mold and leaves a streak-free shine. Be sure to pay attention as to whether the lemon juice should be diluted with water or used straight up. Bonus: Lemons smell fantastic!

MICROWAVE CLEANER

2 cups water

¼ cup lemon juice

Combine the water and lemon juice in a microwave-safe glass dish. Microwave on high for six to eight minutes (depending on oven size and power). The steam from the solution will loosen crusty food particles on the interior so that wiping up is a breeze.

LEMON STAIN REMOVER

This is for kitchen and bathroom surfaces. Combine equal parts lemon juice and salt into a paste and scrub the stain, but not too hard. Rinse well when the stain is gone. Since lemon juice is a bleaching agent, don't use this mixture on colored laminate surfaces or wood.

Salt

In homemade cleaning products, salt is mainly used as an abrasive—and it's very effective. Be sure not to scrub too hard when using salt; doing so might damage the surface you are trying to clean. Salt is also a desiccant, so it's good for absorbing liquids and cutting grease.

STICKY STOVE CLEANER

Regardless of whether the overflow is on the bottom of your oven or on top of the stove, sprinkle a thick layer of salt on the spill while it's still liquid—or dampen with water if it's dry and stuck on. When the surface has cooled, wipe up the spill with a sponge.

CUTTING BOARD SANITIZER

Make a solution in a spray bottle using 2 tablespoons of salt per 1 quart of warm water (warm water dissolves the salt better than cold water does). Shake until the salt is dissolved, then spray on the cutting board until it is saturated with the solution. Allow to dry naturally, or wait 5 to 10 minutes and wipe with a clean cloth. The salt dissolves the cell walls of bacteria, killing them.

Olive Oil

Olive oil can be part of a natural cleaning routine, but there are some things to consider first. Using lower-grade oils for cleaning saves money (keep the extra-virgin grade for salads!). Since olive oil is a relatively heavy oil and tends to leave a residue, avoid using it on wood floors, where it would be a slipping hazard (even thorough wiping isn't enough to remove it all).

A WORD OF WARNING

Do *not* use olive oil for any kind of cleaning if your house is on a septic system. The oil residue can smother the necessary bacteria that live in the septic system, leading to backup problems.

WOOD POLISH

Chemical furniture polishes are mostly silicone, which can dull the finish over time. Instead, dab a clean cloth into a mixture of 1 cup of olive oil and ½ cup of lemon juice, and wipe a little bit of it over furniture, sides and legs included. Afterward, use another clean, soft cloth to go over the oiled surface and buff it to a polished, environmentally friendly shine.

You can also blend the mixture in a spray bottle, but be sure to spray the mist onto a soft cloth and NOT directly onto the furniture. Clean and buff as described above.

LEATHER REPAIR

Olive oil—and other cold-pressed oils—can repair scratches, restore color, and add luster to worn-out leather seats, shoes, and other items. Just dab a little onto a soft cloth and gently rub it in.

CLEAN AND SEASON CAST IRON

Make a scrub using coarse salt and olive oil to remove stuck-on food and other debris and keep your cast-iron skillet's surface seasoned, too.

Club Soda

Club soda is just carbonated water, sometimes with a little salt added. For cleaning purposes, look for the kind with sodium on the ingredients list as the carbonation helps the salt clean better by oxidizing the reaction (like "oxy" cleaning products do).

STAIN REMOVER

Club soda is often used on cocktail and wine stains because it's available at bars, but it is also effective on other organic liquid stains (food, grass, fruit juice, pet stains, etc.). Douse the stain with straight club soda, then dab the area with a clean cloth. Avoid rubbing, because that will only spread the stain and push it further into the material.

Other Natural Recipes

You can do so very much without chemicals in your life. Here are a few alternatives, some of which might be a little unexpected!

DISHWASHER RUST REMOVER

Dishwasher interiors can get rusty due to mineral buildup. Put a package of dry Kool-Aid lemonade mix in the soap dispenser, then run a hot wash cycle. Your dishwasher will sparkle and smell great.

SILVER POLISH

Mix cornstarch and a little water into a thick paste. Cover the silver in the mixture and let dry. Buff off the solution with a dry, soft cloth to reveal a brilliant shine.

REMOVE TREE SAP AND GOO FROM AUTO PAINT

Rub a little mayonnaise onto each spot (don't use anything abrasive like a scouring sponge) and let it sit for 5 to 10 minutes. Afterward, wipe it off with a soft rag. Wash the car as usual. Try this technique with road tar and stuck-on insects as well.

ESSENTIAL OIL ROOM SPRAY

Add 12 to 15 drops of pure essential oil to ½ cup of white vinegar and 1⅓ cups of water. Put in a spray bottle (preferably glass) and spray into the air or on fabrics as needed. An aromatherapy diffuser is an easy way to use essential oils; follow the manufacturer's directions. Some popular essential oils include bergamot, vanilla, ylang-ylang, clove, geranium, tea tree, lemon, peppermint, cedarwood, sandalwood, and lavender. Avoid essential oils containing chemical additives.

NATURAL HOT POTPOURRI

½ cup water

2–3 quarter-inch slices of lemon or orange

6–10 cinnamon sticks

¼ teaspoon whole cloves

10–12 drops essential oil (eucalyptus works well)

In a small saucepan or pot, combine the water, citrus slices, cinnamon sticks, cloves, and essential oil. Bring to a boil and let simmer over low heat; be sure to check that the pan doesn't burn dry. The aroma is warm, relaxing, and great to use year-round.

These ingredients (with the exception of the essential oil) can be reheated three or four times before they need to be replaced with fresh ones.

Maintaining Your Yard Naturally

Gardening is one of the most popular pastimes in the world, whether it's growing flowers for beauty, vegetables for food, or herbs for health and cooking. Unfortunately, gardening is also a source of some of the worst chemical contamination in our lives. Fungicides, pesticides, herbicides, and fertilizers have all passed from commercial agriculture to home garden use—mainly as a result of advertising.

Advertising has created unrealistic expectations surrounding the way things are supposed to look, and our landscapes are no different. Manicured lawns, sculpted shrubs, and spotless beds are the norm in magazines, on TV, and even on gardening websites. What's rarely mentioned is the amount of work and chemicals it takes to maintain this appearance on a daily basis. If we let go of these largely unrealistic ideas, we can create a green habitat that is easier to maintain, chemical-free, and a sanctuary not only for you and your family but for some local fauna as well.

While the benefits of making these changes to the health of our families and the environment are obvious, altering our behavior and expectations is going to take some work.

Weeds are a good example. In general, a weed is simply any plant growing in a spot where it isn't wanted. There are lots of lists of undesirable weeds, but many plants on lists like these are actually native growers that are essential to the health and survival of wildlife and beneficial insects. Dandelions are one example: Widely thought of as a spoiler of the perfect lawn, dandelions (while not native) are a vital early spring food source for pollinating insects such as honeybees. Poisoning lawn weeds such as dandelions, as well as many other native flowering species, is contributing to the critical decline of honeybee populations around the world.

Dealing with Weeds

If you're devoted to killing weeds, there are ways to do it that are much less harmful to the environment and beneficial insects. Pulling weeds by hand is generally the safest solution to weed control, though if there are a lot of weeds, pulling them all can be hard work. It's also difficult to pull up plants with deep roots or underground runners, such as crabgrass and ground ivy. Here are some other natural ways of dealing with annoying weeds.

DEFINE YOUR TERMS

Pesticides: *Pesticide* is a generic term for a substance that eliminates pests—whether animal, insect, fungus, or plant. Many people, however, use the term to refer specifically to chemicals sprayed on food crops to kill insects (which are technically **insecticides**) or weeds (which are really **herbicides**). Generic use of the term *pesticide* can sometimes cause a lot of confusion. Regardless, pesticides are a growing health concern among world populations, both human and wild. Even "organic" foods, which are grown without the direct use of chemicals, are being contaminated by pesticide drift through the air or by seepage into groundwater. Not only are pesticides harming our bodies and our environment, but many pesticides are often nonessential when it comes to saving crops from insects or disease.

1. Mow Less

A healthy lawn should never look like a golf course. Without daily maintenance, this kind of pristine surface is easily overrun with weeds and is subject to drying out due to the extreme shortness of the grass. Instead, set the mower blade high and mow only as needed—3½ to 4 inches. Keeping grass taller helps keep weeds at bay by shading the soil so that weed seeds can't germinate. Mow as needed, with the bag attached. If you have a lot of weeds, removing the clippings prevents weed seeds from spreading throughout the lawn. However, leaving the grass clippings on weed-free lawns after cutting helps fertilize the grass and improve soil structure.

2. Burning

Burning weeds (also called "flame weeding") involves hitting weeds with an intense burst of heat, but not setting them on fire. Heat damages the cell walls of the weed. Use a handheld torch, available from major garden centers or online (a butane cooking torch or even a cigarette lighter will do in a pinch); run the flame over each plant a couple of times. This is most effective when the weeds are still small. Don't set them on fire—just burn them a bit. Repeat the process every few days for a week or so, until the weed stops regrowing. Burned weeds don't die right away; they may take a few days to wilt and die.

3. Mulching

Covering bare soil has some great benefits: It moderates soil temperature, keeps the soil moist, gives plants added nutrients—and keeps away weeds. You can use a variety of materials to mulch, such as wood chips, pine needles, or leaves; inorganic mulches such as gravel are also good, particularly in dry climates or where drainage is important.

LANDSCAPE FABRIC

Some fabrics are much better than others at preventing weed germination. Choose a high-quality densely woven fabric, and then install it properly—which is easier said than done. Follow the installation instructions carefully, ensuring that you are putting the proper side of the fabric faceup. Getting it wrong means that water won't be able to penetrate the fabric and your plants will die, while weeds will be able to sprout right through the material. Your beds may end up in worse shape than they started. Avoid plastic, because it becomes brittle and breaks down fairly quickly, adding toxic chemicals to the soil.

Organic mulches—that is, those made from formerly living materials—include grass clippings and straw (the latter might be better used in beds away from public viewing). Alternatively, newspaper and cardboard are excellent mulches for smothering weeds across large areas, and are best covered with another mulch like bark chips or gravel to keep them weighted down.

Layer organic mulches a *minimum* of 2 inches deep over the soil surface to effectively suppress weed growth (though some weeds will grow eventually); renew mulch every few years as needed, layering new mulch on top of the old. If you use newspaper, put a thick (minimum 3 sheets) layer of newspaper down on your garden beds with holes cut out for the plants you want to grow. Cover the paper with 3 to 6 inches of other mulch to keep it from blowing away. The paper will keep moisture in the soil, and water will still be able to penetrate it to nourish plants.

4. Boiling Water

Using boiling water to kill weeds is so effective that one farming manufacturer has developed a machine that can be towed behind a tractor, and sprays hot water—instead of herbicides—onto the soil. The machine reportedly works every time.

Pour the boiling water directly onto weeds, being careful to apply only to weeds, not plants you want to keep. This method works best for weeds in sidewalks or driveways, away from the roots of desirable plants. Boiling water causes cell damage to underground roots, killing the weed—but it will also kill any other plant it touches. For weed control on larger patches, other methods are more suitable.

5. Shade

Shading weeds is a time-consuming process, but it works for large patches of ground. Shading weeds has an effect that's similar to mulch: You cut off the light source so that the weeds can't grow.

For weeds that are just starting to grow, cover them with a light-blocking material like newspaper or fabric. Pin the edges of the material to the ground with landscape staples, or weight it down with stones. If weeds are already tall, suspend cheap household or landscape fabric above weeds to block out the sunlight. For example, string a tarp between two trees, or use garden hoops or lawn chairs to drape fabric across to strongly shade the area.

Natural Weed Killer Recipes

You don't need harsh chemicals to control weeds in the landscape. A quick trip to the grocery store will provide the materials for easy homemade recipes that are effective natural weed killers.

For each of the following recipes, just mix all the ingredients and pour into a
continued

LITTLE-KNOWN PESTICIDE FACTS

Below are some facts about pesticide use by large companies. While there's not much an individual can do to impact the agricultural practices of these companies, knowing what goes into food production can sow the seeds for growth and activism later down the road.

1. The EPA is downplaying the hazards of pesticide use.

A particular group of pesticides known as organophosphates are proven endocrine disruptors and neurotoxins. Dow Chemical's chlorpyrifos, which has been *banned* in household products since the early 2000s, is still being sprayed on most food crops in the United States—at a rate of 5 million pounds per year. It is the second most commonly found pesticide residue on food. Three recent university studies spanning 14 years have proven chlorpyrifos causes organ damage, mental disorders, learning disabilities, autism, and lowered IQ numbers. The EPA has been notified of these results, but still has not moved to ban the compound completely.

2. Pesticides are contaminating organic farms.

More volatile toxic pesticides come into use in agricultural fields nationwide every year, partly as a response to the increasing resistance of organisms to conventional sprays. Organic and family farms are fighting a losing battle to shield their certified produce from the massive drift cloud that often arrives from neighboring standard farm operations.

Part of the problem also stems from genetic modification of crops that have pesticides spliced into their DNA. These compounds, since they are in the plants' genes, are also present in the pollen and the seeds, which do not recognize property boundaries. Pollen drifts and pollinates organic crops, whose offspring now have the pesticide-modified genes in them.

3. Banned pesticides are still poisoning us.

It is common in chemical manufacturing for a compound to be developed, undergo minimum required testing, then enter widespread use—only to have serious side effects emerge later. Only then, after the damage is done, are restrictions put on the product. Pesticides tend to be *persistent* organic toxins, meaning they linger. At Washington State University, researchers took another look at methoxychlor, a pesticide banned in 2003. They discovered that a person alive today could be suffering kidney disease, ovarian or reproductive disorders, and even obesity simply because their great-grandparents were exposed to the product. Disease incidence spanning up to four generations makes it apparent that chemical toxins need much stricter regulations than are currently employed.

4. Pesticide exposure causes Parkinson's disease.

The University of Colorado conducted a long-term study that looked at statewide rates of pesticide exposure and compared them with rates of Parkinson's disease (a progressive neurological disease)—and a significant correlation was revealed. By tracking atrazine (a common pesticide used across the United States) in contaminated groundwater, researchers found that Parkinson's rates surged from 4 percent up to 40 percent as atrazine contamination increased.

5. Pesticides are a problem for essential pollinators.

Most people don't know that monarch butterfly numbers have declined a staggering 90 percent in just the past 20 years. Their winter habitat in Mexico has decreased from 45 acres in 1996 to a mere 1.7 acres in 2013. Monarch larvae feed only on milkweed plants, but milkweeds are roadside weeds found in cornfields and along fence lines, where glyphosate has wiped them out. Monarchs are crop pollinators and are an important component of food crop sustainability.

More people are aware of how honeybee populations around the world have crashed, with as many as 50 billion bees—over seven times more people as there are on Earth—estimated to have been wiped out in a few months during the winter of 2018–19. This equals 30 percent of all US bee colonies, and is the highest number recorded since the annual survey began in the mid-2000s.

The United States is still spraying the pesticides clothianidin, imidacloprid, and thiamethoxam on more than 140 million acres of cropland every year—despite these compounds being connected to the collapse of bee colonies, and the subsequent banishment of the compounds across the European Union.

While herbicides like glyphosate target plants and not bees, genetically modified crops resistant to Roundup have the herbicide molecule spliced into the plant's DNA. So, every part of the plant—including the pollen and nectar that the bees gather and feed to their young—contains the herbicide. This has caused succeeding generations of bees to be weakened, and eventually die. Combine this problem with decreasing availability of noncommercial hive sites and much lower numbers of native flowering plants (which we've labeled "weeds"), and bee populations are circling the drain.

1-gallon handheld sprayer, which you can find at most garden centers. It should have a long nozzle and a push pump to build up the pressure and dispense the weed killer. The nozzle helps target only weeds. Avoid getting these mixtures on plants you want to keep—they will severely damage or kill those plants as well. These mixtures work best on weeds in concrete cracks or mulched beds. Weeds should shrivel up quickly, as the salt and sun make it hard for the weed to take in enough water to keep from wilting.

WEED KILLER 1

1 gallon white vinegar

1 cup salt

1 tablespoon liquid dish soap

Combine the ingredients in a spray bottle or long-handled sprayer. Spray on weeds when it's sunniest out.

WEED KILLER 2

1 gallon white vinegar

1 cup Epsom salt

30 drops clove essential oil

20 drops pine essential oil (optional)

Combine the ingredients in a spray bottle or long-handled sprayer. Spray on weeds when it's sunniest out.

WEED KILLER 3

1 gallon white vinegar

1 cup boric acid laundry detergent additive (20 Mule Team Borax can be found in most grocery stores)

1 tablespoon natural dish soap

This recipe is the most pure and natural of the bunch. Combine the white vinegar, boric acid (a natural salt) laundry detergent additive in a spray bottle or long-handled sprayer. Add natural dish soap (most regular liquid dishwashing fluid contains detergents and petroleum distillates), which acts as a surfactant and breaks down the waxy covering of the weed, making it more susceptible to drying out. Spray on weeds when it's sunniest out.

WEED KILLER 4

For this recipe you'll need citrus oil with d-limonene, a food-grade compound sourced from citrus peels; liquid concentrate of d-limonene is available online or at some health food stores, but costs $20 to $30 for a 32-ounce bottle. It's not cheap, but because it's food-grade, it can be used as a health supplement or substitute for citrus essential oils. Combine ½ cup of the oil, a 15-ounce bottle of real lemon juice (not chemically preserved reconstituted juice), and 3 quarts of water in a spray bottle or long-handled sprayer. Shake well and spray or pour on weeds.

OK Commercial Weed Killers

If homemade solutions don't work or you don't have time to make them, here are some safer commercially available alternatives to toxic chemical herbicides:

- Doctor Kirchner Natural Weed and Grass Killer: nonselective (kills everything it touches)
- Espoma Organic Weed Preventer: kid- and pet-friendly; selective systemic made from corn
- Green Gobbler 20% Vinegar Weed Killer: wildlife safe; kills by desiccation
- BioSafe Weed Control Concentrate: listed as organic by the Organic Materials Review Institute; kills everything within hours
- If the above weed killers are too expensive and the other methods are too time-consuming, or you found them ineffective, don't sweat it. Take a look at the ingredients of other effective, less-green weed killers in your price range and try to avoid glyphosate, atrazine, diquat dibromide, picloram, 1,4-dioxane, and 2-4-D, all of which are toxic, problematic chemicals.

Mosquito Management

DEET is the most common mosquito repellent in widespread use. Originally developed in the 1940s for wartime use, DEET contains chemical components that can potentially trigger the growth of cancerous tumors and cause seizures in mammals (including humans). Other side effects include breathing difficulties and temporary burning of the skin and mucous membranes. DEET is hazardous to small children and pregnant women, as it may have immune-suppressing and neurotoxic effects.

Not all mosquitoes are repelled by DEET. Additionally, the product can slowly dissolve nylons and plastics (like those in synthetic fibers). Spraying it on these types of fabrics may damage your clothing over time and lead to the shedding of even more microfibers in the washing machine, and eventually to the oceans. Instead, try some essential oils to ward off these and other pesky insects.

Lemon Eucalyptus Oil

Lemon eucalyptus oil (also sometimes called PMD) is a distilled by-product of lemon eucalyptus, and is not to be confused with regular eucalyptus essential oil. In high concentrations (above 30 percent), lemon eucalyptus oil has been shown to provide the same amount of protection for the same length of time as DEET-derived sprays. It's one of the few natural ingredients included on the EPA's (as well as the Australian Pesticides and Veterinary Medicines Authority's) list of effective natural mosquito repellents.

Lavender Oil

Lavender oil, like the oils of thyme and oregano, is naturally toxic to certain mosquitoes and ticks, while having a natural antioxidant and calming effect on humans.

Thyme Oil

Thyme oil contains *monoterpenes*, naturally derived plant extracts that have been shown to be as effective as DEET at repelling mosquitoes. Some studies have found that monoterpenes may repel bugs for longer than DEET.

Catnip Oil

While catnip maybe be your kitty's favorite herb, researchers at Rutgers University have created a version of catnip that not only keeps cats engaged longer, but also has higher concentrations of mosquito-repelling essential oils. Catnip is a member of the mint family, and has been shown to block the feeding receptors of mosquitoes in multiple ways, effectively making us invisible to the bugs.

Geraniol

Geraniol is naturally derived from rose and citronella oils. Citronella is a plant-derived oil often used in backyard tiki torches and anti-bug candles. Added to a vanilla extract, the two are a powerful combo for naturally repelling mosquitoes—even remaining 70 percent effective up to an hour after application. Research shows that geraniol can also repel ticks better than DEET.

A WORD OF WARNING

Do not apply undiluted essential oils directly to skin; burning or photosensitivity may result. Dilute the essential oil with water and/or alcohol, then dab on areas that won't receive sun exposure; alternatively, spray on clothing.

Other Oil Options

Other essential oils that make effective bug repellents include peppermint, holy basil, rosemary, and tea tree. Peppermint (and geranium as well) contains *menthone*, a monoterpene that can repel mosquitoes up to 90 percent as effectively as DEET for as long as two hours. At similar concentrations, DEET repelled insects for only 15 minutes. Extracts of cumin and cinnamon are also proven effective. Some studies have shown that eating foods like garlic, vinegar (for example, as salad dressing or pickles), lemongrass, and chile peppers may help prevent mosquito bites as well.

ESSENTIAL OIL BUG SPRAY

8–10 drops lemon eucalyptus oil

8–10 drops citronella

8–10 drops pure vanilla extract or vanillin (a vanilla extract alternative made from wood pulp)

16 ounces distilled water

1–2 tablespoons witch hazel (optional)

Mix the lemon eucalyptus oil, citronella, and either pure vanilla extract or vanillin in a 16-ounce glass spray bottle. Fill the rest of the bottle with distilled water. Add 1 to 2 tablespoons of witch hazel (if desired) and apply to itchy skin. Shake the bottle before each use, as the water and oil will naturally separate with settling.

In general, the higher the essential oil concentration, the more repellent it will be. Remember to always dilute essential oils and never use them directly on the skin in undiluted form. Also, natural bug sprays made with essential oils will lose efficacy fairly quickly due to evaporation, so reapply every hour or so.

ALCOHOL-BASED BUG SPRAY

1 pound dried wild sage

12–14 ounces dried clove basil (or other fragrant basil)

1 quart 50 percent ethanol or 100 proof alcohol such as vodka or tequila (NOT methyl alcohol/methanol)

Distilled water

In a food processor (or blender on a low setting), combine the sage and dried clove basil (or other strongly flavored basil), grinding until fine. Add the dry mixture to the ethanol or alcohol. Let sit for at least 3 days, shaking the mixture several times a day. The alcohol will extract the essential compounds from the plants, eventually evaporating. Strain the plant bits out of the mixture by pouring through cheesecloth into a 16-ounce glass bottle. Add distilled water to fill the remainder of the bottle.

A WORD OF WARNING

Isopropyl or rubbing alcohol can be used in place of the ethanol, but methanol cannot. Do not drink any mixture made with rubbing alcohol, as it is toxic to humans.

OTHER WAYS TO AVOID MOSQUITO BITES

A good way to avoid mosquito bites is to deter them from hanging out in your yard in the first place. Here are a couple landscaping solutions to keep the biters at bay:

Landscape Effectively

Certain plants can help repel bugs, so place a few around your yard and home to help ward off mosquitoes. Citrus plants such as lemon and orange have been used to repel bugs in regions prone to mosquito-borne illnesses, such as Tanzania. Eucalyptus trees are also effective, though they have certain growth requirements. Citronella (*Cymbopogon nardus*, also *Pelargonium citrosum*, a geranium) is sold under the common name gopher plant, mosquito plant, or citronella grass; the source of true citronella is a matter of some debate in the horticulture world.

Keep Grass Mowed Short

This also deters mosquitoes, as does eliminating sources of standing water in the landscape. Mosquitoes lay their eggs in standing water, so make sure that your pots (indoor and outdoor) have good drainage and that water doesn't collect in saucers underneath the pots. If you have a birdbath, a water feature, or a pond in your yard, consider installing a small solar-powered fountain or agitator to keep the water moving so that mosquitoes can't lay eggs. Live fish (if the pond is big enough) will eat mosquito larvae that do hatch.

Tips for Your Greenest Outdoor Life

Green living is meant to be experienced in green spaces! Use the following tips, tricks, and lifestyle hacks to put down your roots.

Start a Vegetable Garden

Imagine growing your own food right outside your kitchen door, and always having fresh herbs and veggies at hand for dinner. Afterward, the scraps go out to the compost bin to one day help grow more vegetables.

Starting a garden isn't just something for those with a huge backyard. Growing in containers is a great way to garden if you don't have much yard space. Everything from tomatoes and lettuce to peppers and herbs all do great on a sunny patio or front porch. You can even grow some of them under lights indoors or on a brightly lit windowsill.

Growing your own produce lets you control which chemicals (if any) it's exposed to, and homegrown just tastes better. There's nothing like a veggie still warm from the sun!

Save Water

There are so many ways to save water outside your home. The Australians, who live in a very dry climate and do all they can to save water, use everything from buckets in the shower to huge tanks outside their homes to collect and reuse water. Water collected from showers and washing machines (not from sewage) is called "gray water" and is suitable for watering gardens as long as it doesn't contain high levels of detergents or phosphates.

Installing a water tank or rain barrel that can catch rainwater runoff from your roof and gutters is a great way to help the environment. Connect a hose from the tank or barrel and water your garden whenever it needs it—which is especially handy if your region is affected by drought or water restrictions.

Plant Trees

Around the world, there is a great movement afoot to plant more trees. As mass deforestation of the Earth is taking place, every tree replaced is an improvement in our environment and our lives. From the Nature Conservancy's Plant a Billion Trees program to German millennial-founded Plant-for-the-Planet's Trillion Tree Campaign, global groups are helping restore vital tree cover to our world.

If you've got the room, plant a tree or two. Ask at local nurseries or garden centers about the tree species best suited for your area and your needs. Whether you want cooling shade, food for wildlife, or fruit for the table, there's a tree species to suit every need and environment type. There are lots of small trees that do well in containers—even dwarf fruit trees—so be adventurous when thinking about trees.

Grow Grass Greenly

Getting local advice is again going to be your best bet. Head to your local nursery and ask for the type of lawn grass that grows best in your location and requires minimal watering and chemical fertilizers. Sometimes these will be native grasses, but there are also some special grasses designed to thrive with very little water. These do well in drought-stricken regions but will also help cut down on the amount of time spent watering by hand. Consider having your kids checked for possible allergies to different grasses before planting. And of course, avoid chemical weed killers and fertilizers. Locally adapted grass species shouldn't need much of these anyway, so using them will make lawn care easier.

When you're done mowing, throw the clippings on the compost pile, secure in the knowledge that they are free of any contaminants. Then, sprawl out on your chemical-free lawn and take a well-deserved nap.

* * *

Actions You Can Take

SEED

Clean your environment and avoid toxins. The first thing to tackle when starting a cleanse is to rid your home environment of harmful toxins, both chemical and biological. Clean the floors, beds, and upholstery. Use a wet cloth to wipe up dust instead of sweeping, which can spread dust particles into the air and throughout the house.

SPROUT

Reduce exposure to toxins. Make your own natural cleaning products. A mixture of distilled or purified water, lemon juice, peppermint essential oil, and vinegar makes a natural disinfectant. Mix baking soda with water and lemon juice for a good disinfecting scrub. Replace cosmetics and hygiene products with organic versions. For example, coconut oil is a nice substitute for skin and hair care products.

TREE

Think about how you put down roots. Do not build or purchase housing built in areas subject to soil erosion. People love hillsides because of the views, but clearing hills and river bottoms for housing can have disastrous effects. If you already own land, avoid pesticides and chemicals when landscaping, plant trees for future generations, and consider setting the property aside for conservation purposes. This means that the land won't be developed in the future. See an accountant if you have tax or estate concerns.

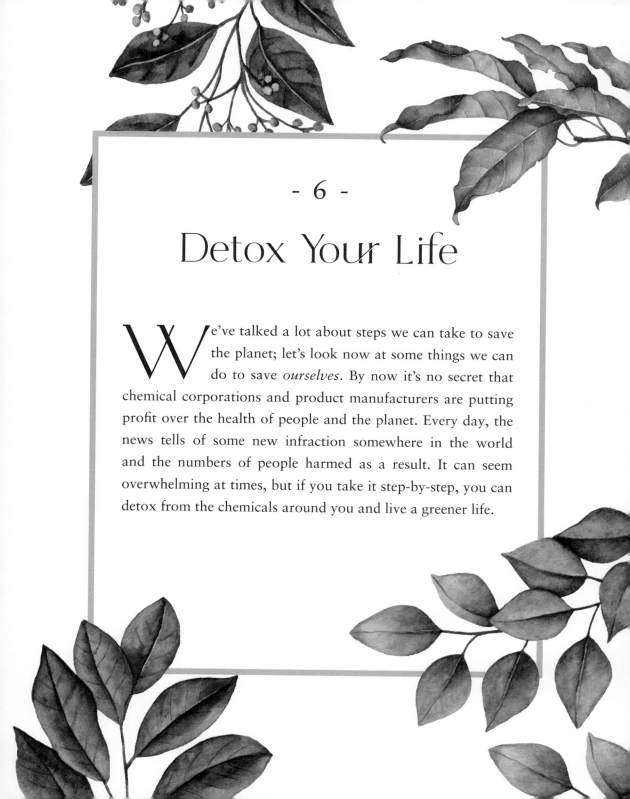

- 6 -

Detox Your Life

We've talked a lot about steps we can take to save the planet; let's look now at some things we can do to save *ourselves*. By now it's no secret that chemical corporations and product manufacturers are putting profit over the health of people and the planet. Every day, the news tells of some new infraction somewhere in the world and the numbers of people harmed as a result. It can seem overwhelming at times, but if you take it step-by-step, you can detox from the chemicals around you and live a greener life.

Going Toxin-Free

It is important to detox your family, your home, and your life. By learning what is toxic around your home and what is going into your body, and by teaching your children how to live a healthy lifestyle, you can transition to a life with fewer toxins.

Detoxing your life will take some time and will require a certain mind-set. Some toxins are easy to remove, but others are seamlessly woven into the fabric of our lives and can be harder to avoid. Take time to detox and let yourself incorporate the toxin-free mind-set into your day-to-day life bit by bit.

Start, perhaps, first thing in the morning by considering what you put directly into your body. Avoid some of the unhealthy beverages like artificial fruit drinks, sugary drinks, energy drinks, and nonorganic coffee. Reduce the number of times that you go out to eat. Most restaurants use excessive amounts of salt and fat and aluminum cookware to cook their food. Instead, spend family time cooking a nice organic meal to share together. Avoid processed food, and reduce the amount of gluten and red meat that you're consuming in your diet. There's no need to remove them entirely (both can be good in moderation!), but consider how much is good for you and how much is too much. As you build up your detox wherewithal, you can move through your kitchen, looking at the ingredients lists for toxic substances to familiarize yourself with the types of products that should be avoided at the supermarket going forward.

Organic Products

Despite the guidelines put out by the US Department of Agriculture (USDA) for what qualifies a product as organic, American advertising follows no such guidelines and freely uses the word *organic* in any way it sees fit (ditto the terms *natural* and *all-natural*). So, unless the product is actually "USDA Certified Organic" (and shows that certification stamp somewhere on the product packaging), you can't know for sure that the product is free of chemicals, preservatives, artificial colors, and more. To

BIG NUMBERS Of all the chemicals found in personal care products, 884 are toxic. Since 1950, at least 80,000 new chemical compounds have been invented and dispersed into the environment. More than 150 chemicals found in the home are connected to allergies, birth defects, cancer, and psychological disorders. Moreover, until children are approximately 13 months of age, they have no ability to fight the biological and neurological effects of toxic chemicals.

Toxin: Scientifically speaking, a toxin is a poison created in the cells of living organisms that is harmful to other organisms (e.g., botulinum toxin or snake venom). In common usage, a toxin is any substance that comes from outside of a particular organism that is poisonous or otherwise harmful to that organism. Some toxins can be harmful only to certain animals (such as chocolate for dogs), whereas others are universally deadly (botulism.) There are a lot of toxins in the world, but don't hit the panic button just yet. Not all toxins are equally harmful. **Toxicity** is the measurement of how harmful substances are to certain organisms in three ways: acute, subchronic, and chronic. Acute toxicity means that a substance can be harmful after a short amount of time or limited exposure. Subchronic toxicity means that the substance can be harmful if used for more than a year but less than a lifetime. Chronic toxicity refers to substances with frequent and continuous exposure over a long period of time over a life span.

find products that have been USDA Certified Organic, look for that Certified Organic seal.

The lack of government oversight in advertising claims has led to the near-useless designation of "organic" as a description of product safety. In grocery stores, you'll find both regular and "organically grown" versions of many fruits and vegetables. The Environmental Working Group (EWG) puts out a list of the "Dirty Dozen," the fruits and vegetables that are most heavily treated with pesticides. For example, one-third of all nonorganic strawberries contain between 10 and 22 different pesticide residues! These fruits and veggies are the ones worth spending the extra money on for "organic."

The Dirty Dozen
1. Strawberries
2. Spinach
3. Kale/mustard greens/collard greens
4. Nectarines
5. Apples
6. Grapes
7. Cherries
8. Peaches
9. Pears
10. Bell and hot peppers
11. Celery
12. Tomatoes

To illustrate how dirty this dozen can be, 97 percent of commercial spinach samples contain pesticide residues, including the

DEFINE YOUR TERMS

Organic: In a strict scientific sense, organic means anything derived from living matter. Plants, animals, and microorganisms are all organic. In chemistry, organic means any element that contains carbon bonds. Most of us think of "organic" as something that is grown or produced for food or personal products without the use of chemicals, pesticides, or artificial ingredients. It's true that, for the purposes of organic farming certification, the USDA provides strict guidelines for how products must be grown or raised.

insecticide permethrin, which is a neurotoxin. Neurotoxins damage our nerve tissue, affecting the functioning of our entire nervous system. Neurotoxins are also found in cured meats, canned tomato sauce, butter-flavored microwave popcorn (the "butter" flavoring is frequently made from diacetyl, a chemical with a buttery taste that has been linked to the lung condition bronchiolitis obliterans, aka "popcorn lung"), peanut butter, and tuna (which contains the toxic heavy metals lead, mercury, and arsenic).

In contrast to the "Dirty Dozen," the EWG also creates a list of the "Clean Fifteen" products, those with the lowest amount of pesticide residues. These products do *not* need to be bought in "organic" form. (Although these products are clean from pesticides and therefore better for consumption, there are other ecological and sociopolitical factors to consider.)

The Clean Fifteen

1. Avocados
2. Sweet corn
3. Pineapples
4. Onions
5. Papayas
6. Frozen sweet peas
7. Eggplant
8. Asparagus
9. Broccoli
10. Cabbage
11. Kiwis
12. Cauliflower
13. Mushrooms
14. Honeydew
15. Cantaloupe

It's true that thoroughly washing fresh produce removes some of the residue, but pesticides and herbicides may remain in the product due to genetic modification (see chapter 3 for more on GMOs) as well as the natural uptake of contaminants via roots and leaves. This is why USDA organic certification requires that the soil be free of chemical contaminants and fertilizers for at least three years before it can be certified organic. For more information on USDA organic certification, check out the website at www.usda.gov.

How to Protect Yourself from Toxic Metals

Toxic metals are in many common products as well as the foods we eat, the water we drink, and the air we breathe. To protect yourself from them, you first need to establish your baseline. Toxic metal tests can be done by many chiropractors or natural healthcare practitioners using hair, blood, or urine analysis.

Toxic metals are all around us and we need to actively avoid toxic metal exposure. However, *total* avoidance can be very challenging, since the stuff is everywhere. Detoxifying and cleansing your body is the next step in reducing the chemical toxins and heavy metals that affect your health. A sauna is great for heat therapy, which can dissolve toxins in the blood and let you sweat them out.

Aluminum Toxins

When aluminum enters the body, it's absorbed and can accumulate in the kidneys, brain, lungs, liver, and thyroid. Aluminum exposure is common with some occupations like welding and mining. In these industries, vapors may be present and inhalation

CAUTION FOR SIX COMMON TOXINS

Science has come a long way. We've learned the harm that certain chemicals, metals, and other substances have on our body, but sometimes these substances are already deeply ingrained in the market and are hard to eradicate completely. The following toxins should definitely be avoided.

1. Aluminum

Aluminum poisoning has long been recognized, but a recent report adds the claim that toxic deposits of the metal could also lead to an increased risk for Alzheimer's disease. Many personal care products like cosmetics, sunscreen, antiperspirants, and even certain medications can contain it. Some manufacturers use aluminum sulfate in water to improve its clarity.

2. Asbestos in Talc

Common in cosmetics, talc can become contaminated with asbestos during mining and manufacturing. Recently, scientists were able to track the route of asbestos in talc over the course of a year, from the mines to the product to the lung tissue of a deceased mesothelioma patient who had used a talc-containing body powder for years.

3. Cosmetic Toxins in Swimming Pools

A report from late 2014 noted the presence of many personal product compounds in swimming pool water samples. Since swimmers don't normally shower before jumping in, toxins from these products wash off their skin into the pool water. Many of the toxins don't break down in chlorination, as originally believed. These chemicals form an ultra-concentrated toxic "soup" that can be swallowed, breathed in, or absorbed through the skin, particularly children's skin. We can help prevent this by showering before swimming.

4. Bacteria in Cosmetics

In addition to chemical toxins, bacteria may be present in cosmetics. Usually when that happens, a recall takes place. Thousands of products are recalled each year due to this type of contamination, but thanks to lax industry regulations, those recalls are not widely known. The FDA (Food and Drug Administration) doesn't have the authority to order a company to pull a personal product from the shelves. While it can make a request, it's up to the manufacturer to take that step.

5. Microbeads, Again

We've talked about the problems with microbeads (and microplastics) polluting our oceans, but it bears repeating. The magnitude of this issue is staggering, and the lack of attention it's getting in the mainstream press is confounding. Fortunately, many states are limiting or banning them, and there might even be a federal ban on the horizon. We can do our part by putting pressure on manufacturers to eliminate microplastics from products.

6. Heavy Metals

Heavy metals are a critical health concern in our industrial world. Mercury, lead, and cadmium are three metals that can be especially harmful. These toxic metals enter the body through drinking, eating, inhaling, and skin and eye contact. Once in the body, they cause damage at the cellular level by initiating oxidative stress.

can result in a "super absorption" status. Aluminum is one of many toxic metals thought to cause brain abnormalities. Alzheimer's and Parkinson's diseases have been studied for their possible links to aluminum accumulation in the brain.

Products That May Contain Aluminum

Aluminum is ridiculously common. Here are just a few of the products that frequently contain it:

- Antacids
- Anti-diarrhea medication
- Antiperspirants
- Astringents
- Baking powder
- Buffered aspirin
- Cans
- Cookware
- Cosmetics
- Dentures
- Deodorants
- Fireworks
- Foil
- Hemorrhoid medications
- Lipstick
- Nasal sprays
- Processed cheese
- Toothpaste
- Vaccines
- Vaginal douches

Cadmium Toxins

The human body doesn't need cadmium in any amount, and even low levels are toxic. Exposure happens primarily through contaminated foods. However, cigarettes and industrial manufacturing are also sources, as are nickel–cadmium batteries, hazardous waste facilities, and fertilizer. Cadmium is slow to exit the body and the negative consequences of cadmium are disastrous, affecting the cardiovascular and reproductive systems, kidneys, eyes, and brain.

BE CHOOSY ABOUT COOKWARE

Cook food in cast-iron cookware as much as possible, and always bake with glassware. Avoid aluminum foil; instead, store foods in sterilized glass containers. When it comes to personal care products, always look for aluminum in the ingredients list. Most antiperspirants contain aluminum (often listed as aluminum chlorohydrate) unless otherwise specified, but there are many natural substitutes for aluminum-based deodorants and antiperspirants (see page 148 for a recipe with natural alternatives).

Foods That May Contain Cadmium

- Cabbage
- Celery
- Cookies (or any other food that contains chocolate, which may be contaminated with cadmium)
- Organ meats
- Peanut butter and peanuts
- Potatoes and potato products (chips, fries, tots, etc.)
- Shelled seeds

Lead Toxins

Lead has long been known to be hazardous. Drinking water, old buidlings, and tobacco smoke are all potential sources of toxic lead exposure. Dust and flakes from lead-based paint have caused public health nightmares, but fortunately regulations have been able to reduce the exposure.

NO FUN FUNGUS

A poor diet and weakened immune system can also result in the overgrowth of a fungus called *Candida albicans* that takes up residence in your mouth, gut, and skin. This condition is referred to as candidiasis, or a yeast infection. To support a healthy gut, a change in diet as part of a toxin cleanse will help balance levels of candida.

When lead enters the body, it goes into the bloodstream and starts depositing itself in the bones, soft tissue, and brain. It's harmful to children and to the fetuses of pregnant women. Be extremely cautious of exposure to lead.

Products That May Contain Lead

- Antiques
- Cable coverings
- Car batteries
- Ceramics
- Cigarettes
- Crystal
- Paints
- Pesticides
- PVC plastics
- Imported toys and products
- X-ray shields

Mercury Toxins

Mercury is highly poisonous and can be found in thermometers, older dental fillings, seafood, and elsewhere; it can be inhaled or consumed from tainted food. Although mercury has been legislated against, it still enters the environment from sources such as old car batteries in junkyards, manufacturing waste, and some paint residues. Mercury does not break down in the environment or in our bodies. Once it enters the body, mercury gets stored in the kidneys, blood, spleen, brain, liver, bones, and fatty tissues.

Mercury is often a danger to those who work in industrial settings and coal power plants. Vaccine production also involves mercury.

Your body has no use for mercury. Exposure at any amount is toxic. Mercury can seriously affect the nervous system and lead to muscular spasms and even death. Pregnant and nursing women should be particularly cautious, as mercury can contaminate breast milk. Tuna is a primary source of mercury contamination, as are many ocean fish species. Fish absorb mercury from toxic waste in the water. Below are lists of mercury contamination in commercial fish, from the lowest concentrations to the highest

When It's Time to Detox

Your body has a comprehensive detoxification system in which the immune system, respiratory system, skin, intestines, kidneys, and liver all work together. Your skin and respiratory system are the first defense against harmful toxins and chemicals. Once a toxic chemical or biotoxin makes it past these first two body defenses, your immune system takes over. After a filtering and metabolizing process, toxins are expelled from the body as waste.

MERCURY IN COMMERCIAL FISH

When it comes to commercial fish, levels of mercury contamination vary by species.

LOWEST	MEDIUM	HIGHEST
Anchovies, Butterfish, Carp, Clam, Cod, Crawfish, Haddock, Herring, Mullet, Oyster, Perch, Salmon, Sardine, Scallop, Squid, Tilapia, Trout, Whitefish	Bass (Chilean, saltwater, black, striped), Bluefish, Buffalo fish, Grouper, Lobster, Orange roughy, Scorpion fish, Sea trout, Skate, Snapper, Tilefish (Atlantic), Tuna	King mackerel, Shark, Swordfish, Tilefish (Gulf of Mexico)

Over time, the buildup of toxins can make it increasingly difficult for your immune system to work properly. This can weaken your immune system and cause a domino effect of digestive issues, mood swings, loss of mental focus, and sleep disruption. Basically, toxins make you feel unhealthy. Even your body odor can change (an outward sign that your body is telling you that it needs help). "Cleansing" your body is a natural way to help it rid itself of toxins, optimizing its ability to defend against toxins.

Kinds of Cleanses

Cleanses have been performed for centuries. Indigenous Americans often cleansed using methods like fasting and sweathouses to purge the body of unhealthy substances. It wasn't until recently that society started adopting these older, more organic practices to detoxify, lose weight, and stay healthy—without the use of harsh medicines or invasive procedures.

If fasting or a sweathouse isn't for you, flushing toxins from your body using a natural cleanse is a refreshing way to bring back a healthier you on the inside. Fewer toxins in your body will also result in higher energy levels. There are a number of cleanses you can try; most last from three to seven days. Here are the steps to a thorough toxin overhaul:

1. Reduce your exposure to toxins.
2. Improve your diet.
3. Stay hydrated.
4. Take supplements.
5. Get more exercise.

How to Do a Cleanse

Once you have achieved a clean home environment (see the previous chapter), focus on the foods you'll be eating to help cleanse your body. Shifting to an organic vegan or vegetarian diet is essential for a successful cleanse. In order to flush harmful toxins, you

SIGNS THAT YOUR BODY COULD BENEFIT FROM A CLEANSE

- Sugar cravings
- Digestive issues
- Sinus issues
- Acne and rashes
- Fatigue

- Loss of mental sharpness
- Joint and muscle aches
- Depression and anxiety
- Sudden weight loss or difficulty losing weight

- Unpleasant breath and body odor
- Irregular sleep cycles or trouble sleeping

CLEANSE TIPS!

Hop to It

Exercising during a detox or cleanse is a great way to help the body flush out toxins and waste, especially if you break a sweat. An hour of exercise a day (which can be broken up into two 30-minute sessions instead) is ideal. As an added benefit, studies have shown that short bursts of high-intensity training during a detox diet may support weight loss and cardiovascular health.

Hydrate

It is extremely important to stay hydrated during a cleanse. Drink purified or distilled water instead of tap water. To add (pungent!) taste and nutrients, mix 2 tablespoons of raw, organic apple cider vinegar into a gallon of distilled water and shake thoroughly.

must give your organs a rest from unhealthy foods so that they can function at peak efficiency. Foods to avoid include:

- Processed or packaged food
- Sodium-rich foods and MSG
- Meat
- Soda
- Caffeine
- Added sugar
- Artificial sweeteners
- Dairy
- Refined carbohydrates
- Trans fats
- Wheat and gluten

Organic foods that naturally provide antioxidants, vitamins, minerals, and other nutrients can help combat the damage from toxins. Incorporate plenty of probiotic foods to keep your gut microbiota (the single-celled organisms that live in your gut) balanced. Some of the foods that are recommended during a cleanse include:

- Brightly colored fruits: watermelon, strawberries, blueberries
- Citrus fruits: limes, lemons, oranges
- Brightly colored vegetables: broccoli, beets, carrots
- Leafy greens: kale, Swiss chard, spinach
- Seeds and nuts: flaxseeds, sunflower seeds, cashews, pistachios, walnuts
- Distilled or purified water
- Noncaffeinated herbal teas
- Garlic

Adding organic herbs and spices like dandelion, cilantro, eucalyptus, alfalfa leaf, peppermint, milk thistle, and gum acacia is a great way to season your meals and will be beneficial for a healthier and cleaner diet.

Organic Skin Care

Once you've cleaned up your home environment and detoxified your body, it's important to keep it clean by using personal care products that don't contain any of the harmful material you worked so hard to get rid of. Unfortunately, that's not as easy as looking for "organic" on a label.

The majority of consumers who spend the extra money to purchase organic skin care products believe they are getting higher-quality, purer, and more "natural" products. But this isn't always the case. Some organic skin care products still contain the same toxic chemicals as their regular counterparts, so it's critical to read labels and avoid products with harmful ingredients.

There are, however, high-quality genuine organic skin care products that can improve your skin dramatically. Research

A CLEANSE MENU

This guide is an example of what you could eat and drink to help cleanse your body of toxins.

Breakfast
This meal should consist of a bowl of your choice of fruit and a 12-ounce glass of a vinegar–water mix.

Snacks
For a midmorning or afternoon snack, grab a handful of nuts and seeds along with a 12-ounce glass of the vinegar–water mix or a cup of green tea. To avoid unnecessary fat or sodium, make sure the nuts and seeds are not oiled or salted.

Supplements
Performing a cleanse using natural organic supplements is a great way to ensure success. Some supplements are even grouped together in kits that are specifically designed to target certain organs. Check at your health food store for cleanse or detox kits.

Lunch
Lunch should consist of vegetables. Try blending some of your favorite veggies and add some lemon juice for a veggie smoothie. A homemade soup using vegetables, herbs, and spices boiled together in purified water is also beneficial.

Dinner
This meal can be the same as lunch, or you can choose to fast using just the vinegar–water mixture. You can also have a small vegetable or leafy salad with a sprinkling of extra-virgin olive oil.

has uncovered many healthful, organic ingredients that have antioxidant properties that protect skin from damage due to UV radiation and environmental pollutants. Organic skin care products also help the environment: Buying products developed from natural sources without toxic chemicals or preservatives decreases your (and the product's) environmental impact and reduces environmental pollution.

Cosmetic and Skin Care Regulations

Most personal care products contain toxic chemicals that could potentially harm your health, make the effects of aging worse, or cause skin eruptions. Makeup, face creams, moisturizers, and cleansers may offset short-term gains in smoothness and brightness

with long-term problems such as "rebound" skin issues, hormonal disruption, and even increased risks of cancer.

Though companies are required to ensure their products are safe, they are *not* required to do any premarket testing or submit safety data to the FDA before offering a product for sale. In other words, although cosmetic and beauty products are "regulated" by the FDA, there is no FDA approval required for any ingredient or combination of ingredients, except artificial colors. Just a handful of the 80,000-plus chemicals on the market today have ever been tested for safety. The FDA has only ever banned 9 chemicals (in specific formulations) from cosmetic products.

When certain chemicals begin to have harmful effects on people's health or the environment, it's almost always consumer pressure that forces the FDA to take action

continued

INGREDIENTS TO AVOID

Take a look at the ingredients of beauty products that you're thinking about buying. There are reasons to avoid any or all of the following ingredients, but they were also added to products for a reason. Do some research, weigh your options, and test removing or adding products to your routine one at a time so that you can accurately gauge the impact these additions or removals have. Consult your primary care physician or dermatologist if you have any major concerns about the ingredients below.

BHA and BHT

BHA (butylated hydroxyanisole) and BHT (butylated hydroxytoluene) are antioxidant preservatives added to beauty products (as well as foods). BHA is added to cosmetic products that contain fats and oils, especially lipstick and eye shadow, to prevent spoilage. It is considered a likely carcinogen (cancer-causing agent) by the National Toxicology Program. In animal studies, exposure to BHA caused stomach and liver damage, as well as problems with the thyroid and reproductive organs. BHT, a similar compound, was not found to cause cancer, but did cause liver and kidney damage, as well as other toxic effects. Some companies are voluntarily removing BHA and BHT from their products.

Coal Tar and Coal Tar–Derived Colors

Coal tar is a residue from burning bituminous coal and contains hundreds of polyaromatic hydrocarbons (PAHs), such as benzene, toluene, and xylene. It's used in anti-dandruff shampoos, as well as in creams treating skin conditions like psoriasis and seborrheic dermatitis. Studies have found that coal tar can lead to skin, lung, and liver cancers as well as DNA mutations. Coal tar is comedogenic, which means it blocks skin pores (which can cause acne) and increases skin's sensitivity to light. It has been linked to cancerous tumors and non-Hodgkin's lymphoma by the National Cancer Institute but isn't banned in the United States due to conflicts regarding use on hair versus use on skin.

Many colors used in cosmetics were once made from coal tar, though nowadays they are made mainly from petroleum. A number of hair dyes still contain coal tar dyes—usually referred to in the United States as "D&C" or "FD&C," followed by the color and a number (e.g., D&C Red 33).

Formaldehyde

Formaldehyde is a by-product of combustion and is also a known carcinogen. Most studies have centered on the effects of *inhalation* of formaldehyde rather than skin application—but the link to cancer from inhaling formaldehyde is strong enough to recommend avoiding any products that contain it. Formaldehyde and its cousin formalin are found in nail polish, nail polish remover, eyelash glue, hair gel, soap, and other personal care products as a preservative. Exposure to formaldehyde can

occur during salon treatments that involve heat, such as "Brazilian blowout" hair smoothing treatments, even if they *claim* to be formaldehyde-free. This is because formaldehyde is a by-product of the process itself rather than the ingredients. There are also many preservatives (including DMDM hydantoin, diazolidinyl urea, and imidazolidinyl urea) in products such as baby and adult shampoos that release formaldehyde while the product is being used.

Polyethylene Glycol (PEG) Compounds

Polyethylene glycol (PEG) is a synthetic polymer derived from ethylene glycol—the main ingredient in antifreeze. In cosmetics, PEGs are used to create a cream base, and then make it thicker, softer, or more moisturizing. PEG compounds include propylene glycol, polyethylene glycol, and polyoxyethylene. Manufacturers state that PEGs are nontoxic, odorless, colorless, and nonirritating. They are considered inert (i.e., they do not react with other materials). However, PEGs are soluble in many organic solutions—including water—and do not

change the color, odor, or taste of the water. This means that products containing PEGs (which include toothpastes, mouthwashes, and antiseptic rinses) can potentially dissolve the compounds into individual ethylene glycol molecules, creating a poisoning hazard over time. It's also possible that PEGs could be absorbed through the skin in face creams and lotions.

There's some evidence that PEGs are harmful to DNA. Depending on the manufacturing process, PEG compounds may be contaminated with 1,4-dioxane, a chemical the FDA warns may cause cancer, or ethylene oxide, a toxin that interferes with fetal development. Pregnant women should be particularly concerned about PEGs.

Oxybenzone

Sunscreens contain oxybenzone (aka benzophenone-3 or phenyl-methanone), a natural compound from flowering plants, to absorb UV light. Trade names include Milestab 9, Eusolex 4360, Escalol 567, and KAHSCREEN BZ-3.

While the American Academy of Dermatology says oxybenzone is safe, the

Environmental Working Group (EWG), an environmental nonprofit that publishes the Skin Deep Cosmetics Database, has strong concerns that the compound may have endocrine-disrupting properties. One study found oxybenzone caused the creation of excessive amounts of a reactive oxygen species, which can itself cause DNA mutations, cell death, and cardiovascular issues.

Parabens

Many beauty products are currently marketing themselves as "paraben-free" due to increasing consumer concerns regarding the safety of parabens. Parabens are chemical compounds synthesized from benzene and its derivatives, which act as antifungal, antibacterial ingredients in everything from deodorant to toothpaste. Research has shown that parabens can lead to hormone imbalances in the body. Hormonal changes are believed to play a role in the development of breast and reproductive cancers; it has also been demonstrated that parabens can pass from mother to infant through breast milk, and the substances have most recently been indicated as contributing causes to childhood obesity.

According to the EWG's Skin Deep Cosmetics Database, some parabens are worse than others; the strongest evidence for endocrine disruption occurs with isopropylparaben, isobutylparaben, propylparaben, and butylparaben.

Fragrances

Fragrances are added to lotions, body washes, soaps, and thousands of other beauty products to make them more attractive to consumers. Cosmetic companies, however, are not legally required to disclose *which* chemicals are in their fragrances because the components are considered "trade secrets."

Fragrances and perfumes can emit VOCs (volatile organic compounds), formaldehyde, and other toxic chemicals, some of which have been linked to cancer. Some fragrances have been linked to allergic reactions, asthma, and migraine headaches. Products that are labeled "unscented" may still contain so-called *masking agents* that are added to cover up chemical odors. Masking agents are often phthalates, which are known endocrine disruptors. For that reason,

choose "fragrance-free" options whenever possible.

Phthalates

A common ingredient in fragrances as a masking agent, phthalates are endocrine-disrupting chemicals that mimic human estrogen and cause hormone imbalance issues for both women and men. Several studies have found phthalates to also be obesogens, chemicals that alter metabolism and result in weight gain, particularly in children. Phthalates have also been linked to an increased risk of breast cancer.

Siloxanes and Cyclomethicone

Siloxanes are used in cosmetics to soften and smooth skin and hair, to help deodorants glide on easily, and to speed the drying of hair products. Three in particular—cyclotetrasiloxane (D4), cyclopentasiloxane (D5), and cyclohexasiloxane (D6)—are harmful to the environment. D4 is a known endocrine disruptor that interferes with fertility. Cyclomethicone is a mixture of D4, D5, and D6.

D4, D5, and D6 residues accumulate in the liver and fatty tissues of mammals and fish, where they act as antiestrogens and can interfere with female reproductive systems. These

compounds can also cause unnatural enlargement of the liver, and can interfere with the liver's ability to repair and replace its cells.

Polytetrafluoroethylene (PTFE), aka Teflon

Polytetrafluoroethylene (PTFE) is the chemical name for Teflon, Fluon, and other brands most commonly used as a nonstick coating on pots and pans

In cosmetics, PTFE is found in pressed and loose powder, blush, mascara, eye shadow, lip balm, and antiaging cream. While the chemical itself is relatively safe, it can potentially become contaminated with perfluorooctanoic acid (PFOA) during the manufacturing process. PFOA persists indefinitely in the environment and has been detected in the blood of more than 98 percent of the US population.

and leads companies to change product formulations. Become educated about which ingredients are harmful and avoid them.

Healthy Products for Personal Care

While there's a lot of bad ingredients found in commercial personal care products, there are some really good substances out there too. Here are some of the highly recommended ingredients and recipes to make your own products that will keep you smooth, soft, and smelling good.

Jojoba Oil: *Liquid Gold*

Jojoba (pronounced *hoe HOE buh*) is a succulent shrub native to the deserts of the southwestern United States. Also known as coffeeberry or goat nut, it produces seeds that can be rendered into a golden-colored liquid wax, similar in structure to sebum (the waxy substance our skin produces). This is jojoba "oil." Used for hundreds of years by Native peoples, jojoba provides many benefits to skin and hair, including:

- Helps improve acne
- Reduces skin infections
- Helps wounds heal
- Has antiaging properties
- Supports healthy hair growth
- Moisturizes skin and hair

Choose organic, food-grade, cold-pressed jojoba oil without any additives whenever possible. Remember that your skin is the largest organ in your body. If a substance is not clean enough to eat, you shouldn't rub it on your skin. Making your own simple recipes can be a fun activity for you, or with your kids. They also make great personalized gifts for friends and family. Don't be afraid to get creative: If you don't like the smell or texture of one of the oils suggested here, switch it out for a different one that you prefer.

SOOTHING JOJOBA MOISTURIZER

To use jojoba oil to moisturize, simply dab the oil onto your fingers and rub it into your skin. You can also try this method for dry nail beds and cuticles, razor burn, or any other area where needed. If you have oily or sensitive skin, try adding a bit of jojoba oil to your usual moisturizer when your face is feeling dry or tight.

ACNE-FREE CLEAR SKIN

If you're fighting breakouts, jojoba to the rescue! Try this simple recipe to take advantage of its antimicrobial and wound-healing properties:

2 tablespoons jojoba oil

2 tablespoons aloe vera gel

Combine the jojoba oil and aloe vera gel in a container. Mix thoroughly. Take a dime-size amount, rub it together in your hands, and apply over your face while in the shower. Let the mixture stay on for 30 seconds, then rinse off gently. Repeat twice per week for maximum benefit.

NOURISHING JOJOBA LIP BALM

This simple DIY lip treatment uses natural oils to moisturize chapped lips. Adding peppermint oil makes it taste and smell great, and it even repels certain harmful organisms that target the lips.

¼ teaspoon jojoba oil

¼ teaspoon shea butter

¼ teaspoon olive oil

1 drop peppermint essential oil

Mix all the ingredients together in a container. If you experience any difficulty combining them, heat them gently over low heat on the stove, stirring constantly, for no more than 60 seconds. You can also microwave on low (at 50 percent power) for no more than 10 seconds. Watch carefully! Let cool and store in a glass container. Apply as needed.

QUICK RELIEF SUNBURN OIL

While most sun damage is permanent at the cellular level, the good news is that you can use plant oils to soothe and hydrate even damaged skin, and jojoba has natural sun protection factors. Almond oil can also prevent damage from UV radiation, so this oil blend is wonderful for protecting against further sun damage while also soothing skin after sun exposure. **Note:** This oil does not have the same UV absorption capabilities as chemical sunblock, so use caution while out in the sun. The oil is designed for post-sun skin soothing and is not a substitute for sunblock.

1 teaspoon jojoba oil

½ teaspoon argan oil

2 tablespoons almond oil

2 tablespoons coconut oil

Mix the oils together in a container. Gently apply to sunburned skin. Depending on how large the sunburned area is, double the recipe to get the amount needed if necessary.

ALL-NATURAL MAKEUP REMOVER

You can use plain jojoba oil to remove makeup naturally. Put a few drops on a cotton ball or directly onto your fingers and gently massage in, then wipe off with a tissue. If you have time to make this recipe, the vitamin E oil will provide extra moisture. You can get vitamin E oil at a health food store, or poke a vitamin E capsule with a pin and squeeze out the liquid. **Note:** Because the recipe contains water, you shouldn't store it for later use; just make enough for one use at a time.

1 teaspoon jojoba oil

2 drops vitamin E oil

1 tablespoon distilled water

Add all the ingredients to a bottle. Shake well. Gently apply a couple of drops to the area of skin where you want to remove makeup. Use a cotton ball or washcloth to wipe away makeup.

SOFT AND SHINY HAIR TREATMENT

A dry, itchy scalp can be annoying, embarrassing, and even painful. This recipe turns your favorite paraben- and sulfate-free conditioner into a rescue treatment that helps keep your hair soft and shiny, with the added dandruff-fighting (antifungal) benefits of castor oil. In addition, jojoba's wound-healing properties will help repair any areas you've scratched. If you want to boost hair growth or prevent hair loss, maintaining a healthy scalp is important, so make sure you are consuming the proper vitamins and minerals. **Note:** Because of the high oil content of this recipe, you might need two washes to get all the oil out.

- 1 tablespoon jojoba oil
- 1 tablespoon coconut oil
- 3 drops virgin castor oil
- 2 tablespoons hair conditioner
- 3 drops favorite essential oil

Mix all the ingredients together in a container. Massage into your scalp. Leave on for 20 minutes. Then wash your hair thoroughly.

A WORD OF WARNING

Using oils in the shower is a slipping hazard; use caution when rinsing and moving around.

REJUVENATING VANILLA BODY SCRUB

Exfoliation is a key part of any skin care regimen. Sugar scrubs are gentler than salt scrubs because they have round granules without sharp edges. Sugar also dissolves more easily in hot water. However, to exfoliate rougher skin like elbows or feet, use Himalayan pink salt or another coarsely ground salt instead of sugar for best results. If you don't like vanilla, try citrus, eucalyptus, or lavender essential oil instead.

- 1 tablespoon jojoba oil
- 1 tablespoon coconut oil
- 1 teaspoon vanilla extract
- ½ cup coarse organic sugar

Combine all the ingredients in a bowl. Mix them well. The sugar should partially absorb the liquids, forming a paste. Massage into skin and rinse with warm water.

A WORD OF WARNING

Don't store your Rejuvenating Vanilla Body Scrub in the shower, where it might get contaminated with mold or bacteria. Because it contains no preservatives, it does not have as long a shelf life as commercially made consumer products. Additionally, oils present a slipping hazard in the shower or tub. Use caution when exiting either.

Aloe Vera:
The Miracle Burn Reliever

In ancient times, aloe vera was called the "plant of immortality." A true wonder of nature, this spiky succulent has a variety of uses, from treating acne scars and burns to reducing stretch marks. This herbal powerhouse can moisturize, nourish, and soothe. Apply aloe vera gel (the clear, bitter, jelly-like substance inside the leaf) directly onto the skin as a healing salve, or combine it with other ingredients to make unique skin-soothing recipes.

Aloe vera contains more than 75 identifiable nutrients and plant compounds, with various applications for health and healing. This galaxy of powerful healing agents makes aloe vera incredibly versatile for health, wellness, beauty, and cosmetic uses. Its benefits include:

- Moisturizes naturally
- Reduces wrinkles and promotes youthful skin
- Soothes and helps heal burns
- Relieves sunburn
- Helps improve the look of acne
- Promotes skin healing
- Relieves skin itching and irritation
- May help avoid stretch marks
- Supports a healthy scalp

Aloe vera gel has a high percentage of water and is not greasy, making it a very good moisturizer for troubled, acne-prone skin. Antibacterial phenols help speed wound healing and proteolytic enzymes repel microbes that can cause dandruff. Aloe vera has also been shown to stimulate collagen formation, reducing the appearance of wrinkles when smoothed onto skin or taken orally, but consult your primary care physician before consuming. Ingesting aloe vera can cause stomach upset and irritation.

In all of the recipes below, make sure to use either 100 percent pure organic aloe vera gel (if store-bought) or aloe gel taken directly from an aloe plant.

EXTRACTING ALOE VERA GEL

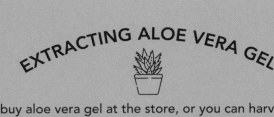

You can buy aloe vera gel at the store, or you can harvest your own from this easy-to-grow houseplant. Here's how:

1. Choose one of the outermost leaves of the aloe plant, making sure you pick one that is at least 8 inches long. This ensures that the leaf is mature and has plenty of gel inside.

2. Cut off the leaf using a sharp knife at the base of the plant. Rinse off and discard any yellow ooze, which is aloe latex.

3. Trim the top one-third of the leaf (the pointy end). This thin part of the leaf does not contain much gel and can be discarded.

4. With the leaf lying flat on a cutting board, cut off the hard, spiny edges on both sides of the leaf.

5. Slice open the green skin down the length of the leaf. You can also use a vegetable peeler to remove it. Underneath, you will see a layer of thick, clear gel at the center. This is the aloe vera gel.

6. Cut the bottom skin off as well and you will have a slab of clear aloe vera gel.

7. Store the gel in a clean, airtight container. Refrigerate and use within one week.

Note: Make sure that you have true aloe vera plant and not agave, which has very sharp, wicked spines. Aloe vera spines are hard but dull-pointed. Agave is often mislabeled aloe vera. If the spines are painful, you've got the wrong plant!

LIGHT SUMMER MOISTURIZER

Aloe vera gel is great for healing summer sun damage while moisturizing. Apply about a teaspoon of it directly to your neck and face, avoiding the eye area. Use in the morning and evening.

ANTIAGING EYE CREAM

1 vitamin E soft-gel capsule

1 tablespoon pure aloe vera gel

Puncture the vitamin E capsule with a pin and squeeze the oil into a small bowl. Add the aloe vera to the oil and mix well. With the pad of your finger, lightly dab a bit of the mixture on the skin surrounding your eyes. Apply nightly before bed.

ALOE VERA, HONEY, AND SEA SALT SCRUB

Use organic, locally grown raw honey, which soothes the skin and naturally wards off allergens and bacteria, among other benefits.

2 tablespoons pure aloe vera gel

¼ cup organic sea salt

1 tablespoon organic raw honey

In a small bowl, combine the aloe vera gel and the sea salt. Mix to create a paste. Add the raw honey and blend well. Use as a face or body scrub, massaging it into the skin and rinsing off with warm water.

ALOE VERA, HONEY, AND ROSE WATER ACNE MASK

Rose water also lends a lovely fragrance to this soothing mask. Alternatively, you can use lemon juice in place of rose water, which brightens and clarifies oilier skins. (Lemon juice can sting if you have sensitive skin, so you might want to avoid using it in that case.)

1 tablespoon pure aloe vera gel

1 tablespoon organic raw honey

1 to 2 teaspoons rose water or organic lemon juice

In a small bowl, combine the aloe vera gel, raw honey, and rose water (or lemon juice) to make a smooth paste. Apply as a mask and keep on your face for no longer than 20 minutes. Rinse with warm water. Use up to three times a week to help with acne.

ALOE VERA AND VITAMIN E MASK

10 vitamin E soft-gel capsules

¼ cup pure aloe vera gel

Break open the vitamin E capsules and squeeze the oil into a small bowl. Add the aloe vera gel and mix well. Massage into affected skin and let sit for at least one hour. Rinse off with warm water. Repeat twice daily.

ALOE VERA AND GROUND COFFEE SCRUB FOR STRETCH MARKS

Coffee grounds exfoliate the skin and may increase blood flow for effective healing.

2 tablespoons pure aloe vera gel

2 tablespoons used organic coffee grounds

Mix the aloe vera gel and coffee grounds in a small bowl until well combined. Apply to stretch marks, massaging into the skin in a circular motion. Let sit on the skin 20 minutes. Rinse well in the shower. Towel dry and moisturize. Repeat three or four times per week.

ALOE VERA AND COCONUT OIL RUB FOR SUPER HYDRATION

Coconut oil offers deep hydration in this skin rub.

⅓ cup pure aloe vera gel

½ cup organic virgin coconut oil

Whisk together the aloe vera gel and coconut oil in a small bowl until fluffy. Massage into stretch marks or extra-dry skin and leave on overnight. Keep the mixture in an airtight container and use nightly for best results.

ALOE VERA GEL FOR MINOR BURNS

On burned skin, apply a thick layer of pure aloe vera gel, about 1–2 tablespoons depending on how large the burn area is. Reapply after the gel dries out. If desired, place a bandage over the aloe vera to hold it in place and retain moisture.

ALOE VERA AND CARROT POULTICE FOR BURNS

This poultice can help prevent scarring from burns. Both carrots and aloe contain vitamins A, C, and E, which assist in healing as well as reducing redness and swelling.

2 organic carrots

½ cup pure aloe vera gel

Finely grate the carrots with a hand grater or food processor. Transfer to a bowl. Add the aloe vera gel and mix well. Apply the mixture to the affected area. Use a bandage around the mixture to hold it in place. Reapply after the poultice dries out, for two or three hours. Gently clean the poultice from the skin, then rinse in the shower. Towel dry and moisturize (honey is good, or use more aloe vera gel). Repeat every other day.

This soak soothes red, itchy, or rashy skin as chlorophyll helps ease skin redness, while the oats contain silica, which studies find improves skin strength and elasticity; oats also relieve itch.

1 cup pure organic aloe vera juice

¼ cup liquid chlorophyll (available at health food stores)

½ cup rolled oats

Cheesecloth bag or nylon stocking

Plug your bathtub and fill it with hot water. As the bathwater runs, add the aloe vera juice and liquid chlorophyll. Add the oats to a cheesecloth bag, tie it closed, and add to the bath. Climb in and soak in the tub for 20 to 30 minutes. Towel dry and moisturize. Toss the oatmeal stocking or recycle if using cheesecloth.

Castor Oil:
An Age-Old Remedy

Despite its strong taste, people have revered castor oil since ancient times. Its earliest mention was in the 6,000-year-old *Papyrus Ebers*, an ancient Egyptian scroll of herbal medicine. Derived from the seeds of the castor bean plant, castor oil was used by the ancient Egyptians to treat eye, skin, and hair conditions, as well as headaches. It was also an important oil in Ayurvedic medicine. During the Middle Ages, this oil's popularity grew in Europe, most notably for its ability to heal skin disorders and digestive ailments. It was also used to end pregnancies.

Fifty years ago, moms everywhere used castor oil as a cure-all for ailments from stomach pain to fever to (its most famous use) easing constipation. Its benefits include:

• Moisturizes skin
• Soothes inflammation
• Helps clear phlegm

A REMEDY WITH A DEADLY COMPONENT

The castor bean plant is the sole species of its genus (*Ricinus communis*); interestingly, castor beans are also the source of the deadly poison ricin. This explains its potent effect as an inducer of miscarriage when the oil is ingested—a use that is absolutely not recommended. The oil is derived by pressing the seeds. An unrelated plant with a similar appearance, false castor oil plant (*Fatsia japonica*), grows in Japan and is sometimes mistaken for the true castor bean plant. Discretion and caution should always be used when ingesting castor oil.

- Resists harmful organisms
- Boosts the immune system
- Heals wounds
- Promotes eye health
- Stimulates hair growth
- Relieves constipation

Ricinoleic acid, castor oil's primary fatty acid, works with the oil's amino acids to nourish and condition skin. Because of its thick texture, castor oil stays put when applied and deeply penetrates the skin's tissue. This is particularly soothing for dry, patchy skin caused by eczema because the anti-inflammatory properties in the oil help reduce itching and discomfort. The antioxidants present in the oil also help prevent skin damage caused by sunburn.

In addition to relieving itchy skin, topical application of the oil reduces inflammation in sore joints due to arthritis. It is also beneficial for gout, muscle tension and sprains, menstrual cramps, and tendinitis. Taking it internally can aid in detoxification by helping the body's lymphatic system flush toxins. It is generally recognized as safe and effective by the FDA for use as a laxative. Make sure to drink a full glass of water when taking castor oil orally.

CASTOR OIL "PULLING" MOUTHWASH

The castor seed protein has antibacterial and even anticancer properties. When combined with ginger, castor oil can significantly reduce the number of bacteria growing in the mouth and can be helpful after oral surgery. This recipe is like "oil pulling," where you swish an oil in your mouth to improve oral

A WORD OF WARNING

Castor seeds contain ricin, which can be toxic even in small doses. The heating during commercial processing *removes* ricin; therefore, **do not attempt to extract castor oil from your own homegrown seeds!** Remain cautious when consuming castor oil internally and never exceed 4 tablespoons (2 ounces) per day. **Do not take castor oil if you are pregnant!** It can cause uterine contractions and induce labor.

Castor oil is not recognized as interacting with other prescription or over-the-counter drugs. External use is usually safe and is an effective way to bring down inflammation. Before using topically, apply castor oil to a small area of your skin to check for any allergic reactions. Consult your healthcare provider if you have a medical condition that involves the digestive tract, or if you have questions about use.

hygiene. (Some alternative medicine practitioners claim that oil pulling can pull toxins from the body, but there is no empirical evidence to support this.) Mix 1 tablespoon of castor oil and ¼ teaspoon of fresh ginger, juiced or minced; swish the mixture in your mouth for 10 minutes; then spit it out—*don't* swallow it. **Note:** Fresh ginger juice is very hot! Test with a tiny bit of the solution before trying the whole dose.

CLEAR THINGS UP

Castor oil packs also work great for detoxification and clearing phlegm from the lungs. To do so, place warm castor oil packs on your chest for one to two hours.

CASTOR OIL PACKS (AKA "PLASTERS")

Castor oil packs are an effective and easy home therapy option for various conditions. They help reduce inflammation throughout the body, help balance the digestive system, relieve headaches and sore joints, and improve overall health. Castor oil packs can be stored in a plastic bag and reused up to 30 times.

Buy cotton flannel cloth. There are specific flannels you can buy for creating castor oil packs, or you can use an old flannel sheet or pillowcase. Make sure the piece is big enough to cover the area where you intend to place the pack, most commonly the abdomen or chest. Avoid wool flannel.

Saturate the flannel cloth in castor oil. You can do this by folding the fabric and placing it into a jar or bowl and pouring in enough castor oil to cover it. You'll want the fabric to be saturated but not completely soaked and dripping.

Cover the flannel cloth with plastic wrap or clean cotton fabric. You can buy special wraparound packs online. You'll want any plastic covering to be larger than the flannel to prevent oil dripping onto the bed, couch, or floor. You can also place plastic underneath you so that if oil *does* drip, it does not get onto surfaces.

Rest the pack on the area of your body you're looking to soothe. Place a hot water bottle over the plastic. Or you can use a heating pad set on low heat. Relax for one to two hours with the castor oil pack in place. This is a great time to practice deep breathing, meditation, or other relaxation techniques. When finished, shower and wash the excess oil from your body. Repeat as needed, up to four times per week.

NATURAL LAXATIVE

If you are constipated, castor oil can provide quick relief. However, there are some caveats to this. The strong taste of castor oil can be a turnoff to some people. You can mix it with warm milk, ginger or chai tea, or orange juice to mask the flavor. Refrigerating the castor oil for an hour can also help decrease the strong taste.

Adults can take 1 to no more than 4 tablespoons of castor oil a day when using it as a laxative, depending on their body weight. Children should take no more than 1 teaspoon. It will generally work within two to three hours, so don't go too far from home. If you are pregnant, avoid castor oil, as it may induce labor.

ACNE TREATMENT

While it may go against everything you've been told about skin care, applying certain oils to your face can actually be good for your skin. Some cosmetics and acne products, like benzoyl peroxide and alcohol-based toners, strip skin of its natural oils, causing inflammation, which leads to pimples. The essential fatty acids in castor oil help restore skin's natural moisture balance, help deter acne-causing bacteria, and clear facial blemishes. It also encourages the growth of healthy skin tissue.

To treat acne, apply 2 to 3 drops of castor oil to your face and massage gently in circular motions. Leave it on overnight and wash your face in the morning with a mild soap or facial cleanser. If you prefer, you can wash it off after five minutes, instead of leaving it overnight.

SCALP CONDITIONER

Castor oil's anti-inflammatory properties can reduce the redness and swelling that contribute to an itchy scalp, and remove the bacteria that cause irritation. A regular treatment regimen can soothe itchy scalp, eliminate dandruff, and improve the appearance of your hair.

Apply 1 tablespoon or so of oil directly to your scalp and massage in well. Leave it on for an hour, and then rinse. You can also leave it overnight (use a shower cap when you sleep) and then rinse out in the morning.

The addition of a couple of drops of rosemary essential oil can increase the antibacterial effect of the treatment, and make the mixture smell better. Adding 2 to 3 drops of high-quality peppermint essential oil will increase blood circulation to the scalp and promote hair growth. Combining coconut or jojoba oil with the castor oil can make your hair shinier. No conditioner is necessary after such a treatment.

JOINT PAIN RELIEVER

The high concentration of ricinoleic acid in castor oil makes it an excellent natural remedy for joint pain. Topical application works effectively for osteoarthritis with no adverse effects. For pain relief, rub the oil directly on your sore joints as often as needed. Apply heat, if desired, using a heating pad on a low setting or a hot water bottle to help your body absorb the oil. Repeat as needed.

FUNGAL INFECTION REMEDY

Castor oil has antifungal and disinfectant properties, making it a useful treatment for athlete's foot and other fungus-related skin infections. Apply small amounts of castor oil directly to the infected area. Just a few applications over one to two weeks should be sufficient.

WOUND TREATMENT

Due to its antibacterial and antimicrobial properties, castor oil can help heal wounds. It also helps ward off infections from many types of bacteria, including *Staphylococcus*, *Streptococcus*, and *E. coli*. Castor oil is commonly used in veterinary care as well, on both open and closed wounds—though you should prevent your pet from licking the wound or ingesting the castor oil.

Apply a generous amount directly to the wound and cover with a bandage. Repeat this process daily until the wound has healed.

SKIN MOISTURIZER

Castor oil is an inexpensive natural antiaging and skin moisturizing remedy. Its monounsaturated fatty acids act as humectants, substances that naturally retain and preserve moisture by protecting the outer layer of skin. It even has wrinkle-reducing properties: It penetrates the skin and boosts the production of collagen, hydrating your skin and making it softer and smoother.

Apply a small amount to your face, neck, and décolletage, and leave overnight. If you prefer, dilute with a carrier oil such as organic grapeseed, almond, or olive oil. It is safe to use this oil in the sensitive under-eye area, but apply only a thin film to avoid having the oil run into your eyes when you lie down. Wash off with a gentle facial cleanser the following morning. Repeat two to four times a week.

Argan Oil:
The Moroccan Wonder

Argan oil is renowned for its outstanding therapeutic and cosmetic benefits. As the name indicates, the oil comes from Morocco, but people around the world have traded it for its healthful properties from as early as the sixth century CE.

Argan oil comes from the tender kernels inside the fruit of the slow-growing argan tree (*Argania spinosa*). When argan oil began its recent boom in popularity, all-female collectives in southwestern Morocco began making the traditional healing oil for sale and export. The women harvested the fruits, smashed the hard shells with stones, picked out the tender kernels inside, and pressed the fruit kernels to retrieve the oil. Planting and tending argan trees also has environmental benefits, by helping to mitigate both climate change and desertification (a process whereby arable land becomes an unusable desert). The main argan forest in southwestern Morocco is now an official biopreserve.

Predictably, the boom in argan oil's popularity has led to aggressive harvesting techniques that injure the sensitive trees. Many larger companies have also pushed out the cooperatives, which have played an important role in empowering women. If you want to support a sustainably harvested, female-empowering product, look for fair-trade argan oil, especially one that is stamped with the UCFA (*Union des Coopératives des Femmes de l'Arganeraie*) seal to ensure that women are receiving a fair price for their knowledge and work.

Argan oil is deliciously smooth and can bring a lovely glow to your skin and hair, but it also may offer benefits inside your body: to the heart, liver, and blood, to name a few. The range of benefits attributed to argan oil includes:

- Improves the appearance of acne and scars
- Promotes elasticity and skin hydration
- Boosts heart health
- Supports liver function
- Supports normal insulin and blood sugar levels
- Protects against cell proliferation (i.e., cancer)

GOOD AND GOOD FOR YOU

In North Africa, it's popular to drizzle roasted argan oil over bread and use it in cooking. Dietary argan oil may be at least partially responsible for the fact that people who follow a traditional Mediterranean diet tend to have less heart disease (northern Morocco abuts the Mediterranean Sea).

Argan oil's omega-6 and omega-9 fatty acid content reduces redness, swelling, and acne-prone skin. While you may feel like putting oil on your skin will make acne worse, the truth is that oils vary substantially from one another, and some (including argan oil) help reduce the irritation and inflammation associated with acne. Those with acne-prone skin are usually deficient in linoleic acid, an omega-6 essential fatty acid, which is found in argan oil.

Fatty acids can also help speed the healing of acne-related scarring and minimize signs of premature aging, such as crow's feet and age spots. Argan oil's comedogenic index of zero means it will never clog the skin's pores or cause breakouts; it can even reduce the greasy appearance of oily skin. And the high level of vitamins A and E deeply nourishes skin. Applying argan oil improves your skin's ability to retain water (as in hydration, not bloat), which, in turn, helps with elasticity. Researchers have also discovered that skin exposed to argan oil experiences changes at a cellular level, allowing it to act as a barrier to dirt, germs, and free radicals. In various studies, dietary argan oil has helped with skin, colon, bladder, and prostate issues.

Make sure the argan oil you use is not only fresh but also certified organic. This will ensure you avoid chemicals such as pesticides. Its odor should smell light, fresh, and nutty. Keep in a cool, dry place (preferably not the bathroom), and store in a dark bottle because exposure to heat and light will cause the oil to oxidize or decay. *If any natural oil smells rancid, throw it out.*

IMPROVE THE APPEARANCE OF STRETCH MARKS

Thanks to its high vitamin A and E content, argan oil keeps your skin well hydrated and improves its strength and elasticity, which in turn helps reduce the appearance of stretch marks. After showering and exfoliating your skin, gently rub a few drops of argan oil onto the hips, thighs, and stomach—the areas most prone to developing stretch marks. Massage the oil into your skin twice a day, including once before bedtime.

MOISTURIZE AND IMPROVE SKIN ELASTICITY

Whether you have oily, dry, or combination skin, you can use pure argan oil as an all-over face and body moisturizer. You can even apply 100 percent pure argan oil directly on your face and lips and around your eyes. You can also soothe razor bumps and ingrown hairs caused by shaving by applying the oil directly to the affected area. For best results, massage it onto your body right after showering or bathing, paying special attention to any dry patches.

You can also add a few drops of argan oil to a carrier oil, like organic olive, coconut, or other seed oil, which helps extend the argan oil.

REDUCE THE APPEARANCE OF ACNE

Argan oil is non-greasy and won't clog pores, so it's a great natural way to add moisture and provide balance to inflamed, acne-affected skin. After you wash your skin and pat it dry, put a few drops of pure oil into your palm and, using your fingers, lightly dab it directly onto concerning areas. Repeat twice daily.

PROTECT AND SOFTEN HAIR

This nourishing, non-greasy oil increases the shine and overall healthy appearance of hair while repairing split ends and smoothing flyaways. By coating the hair shaft, argan oil reduces drying and damage. Argan oil can also help seal in hair dyes, increasing the length of time needed between colorings. It may even promote faster hair growth.

Mix 5 drops of oil with your normal shampoo or conditioner in your hand, massage it into your hair, then rinse it out with warm water. For a deep conditioning boost, coat your hair with 10 drops from the roots to the tips and leave it on overnight with a shower cap over it. This will allow deep penetration into your hair and alleviate frizziness and dryness. In the morning, rinse it out with warm water and style as usual.

MOISTURIZE NAIL CUTICLES

Ward off painful hangnails and other issues associated with poor nail health by applying a few drops of argan oil on your fingernails and toenails. Its antibacterial and anti-inflammatory qualities make it an excellent moisturizer and conditioner for the nail bed and cuticles.

To do a cuticle treatment, first remove all nail polish and rinse your hands and feet thoroughly. Rub a drop of the oil onto each one of your nails and massage it into the cuticles in a circular motion. Leave it on to absorb, covering with gloves and socks overnight if desired.

RELIEVE TIRED FEET

Argan oil can soothe dry, cracked skin on your feet and heels. This hydrating moisturizer is full of antioxidants that can prevent further dryness, soften calluses, and make rough feet soft and smooth again. Slather your feet with as many drops as needed to fully cover the area, and put on a pair of socks for at least 30 minutes (but preferably overnight). After taking off the socks, use a warm washcloth to remove any excess oil from your soles.

Tea Tree Oil: *The Natural Antiseptic*

From antiseptic mouthwash to natural deodorant, tea tree oil has a multitude of uses and benefits. It tends to be pale yellow or colorless with an aroma that is similar to that of eucalyptus or camphor oil, and boasts many medicinal properties.

Tea tree oil is not made from the tea plant (native to China); it's distilled from the leaves of an evergreen shrub called *Melaleuca alternifolia*, which is native to Australia. It has historically been used by aboriginal people for cleaning wounds and other skin concerns. It has antibacterial properties, and researchers have found that tea tree oil targets the cell membranes of bacteria, including *Streptococcus pyogenes* (strep) and *Escherichia coli* (*E. coli*), and destroys them.

Tea tree oil contains the compound terpinen-4-ol, which has anti-inflammatory benefits. One experiment found that terpinen-4-ol could reduce inflammation caused by mites that attack the skin and eyes.

Another benefit of this essential oil is its antifungal properties. It may be helpful in getting rid of fungi such as mold, ringworm, and nail fungus. Researchers have focused on tea tree oil's ability to fight the overgrowth of candida, a type of yeast.

It is also antiprotozoal. Protozoa are single-celled organisms, such as amoeba, that are parasitic and can cause infections such as malaria, which kills hundreds of thousands of people every year around the world. In several studies, tea tree oil has shown that it can kill protozoa.

Researchers have discovered antiviral properties in tea tree oil as well. One study, at the University of Heidelberg in Germany, focused on the herpes simplex virus, which can cause cold sores; tea tree oil decreased the total number of virus particles that could be counted. Another study looked at the ability of tea tree oil to stop the influenza virus from replicating.

HAIR SANITIZER

Some of the most popular tea tree oil uses involve the hair. For instance, one study from the Royal Prince Alfred Hospital in Australia found that a 5 percent tea tree oil shampoo resulted in a 41 percent improvement in dandruff. Not only does the essential oil reduce dandruff, but it may also help suffocate head lice. The shampoo also decreased greasiness and itchiness. According to the National Psoriasis Foundation, some people find relief from scalp psoriasis by using tea tree oil shampoo. You can purchase tea tree oil shampoo or make your own. One of the easiest methods is to add the essential oil to your existing shampoo.

Tea tree essential oil

Your favorite shampoo

Add 2 drops of tea tree essential oil per 2 tablespoons of your shampoo. Make sure the lid is secure on the shampoo bottle. Shake vigorously. Use the shampoo as you normally would. Rinse your hair with water.

COMPLEXION CLEARER

Tea tree oil is present in many skin care products, such as face washes and complexion powders. A study from the Royal Prince Alfred Hospital found that it improved acne with fewer side effects than benzoyl peroxide.

2 drops tea tree essential oil

1 tablespoon raw, organic honey

Mix the ingredients to create a paste. Apply to your face, avoiding your eyes and mouth. Leave it on for 5 to 10 minutes. Wash your face with water.

ECZEMA SOOTHER

Many of the common tea tree oil uses focus on helping skin conditions, including eczema. The soothing actions of terpinen-4-ol in this essential oil can help reduce the irritation caused by eczema.

1 drop tea tree essential oil

12 drops carrier oil such as olive, coconut, jojoba, or almond oil

Mix the oils in a small bowl. Apply to the skin, avoiding the eyes and mouth.

BAD BREATH ELIMINATOR

Usually, bad breath is caused by bacteria, so the antibacterial properties of this essential oil can help get rid of it. When researchers in India compared different essential oils, they discovered that using tea tree oil resulted in a significant reduction of oral bacteria. It's important to remember that you *don't* swallow tea tree oil. It's not safe to ingest because it can cause serious concerns, such as confusion and loss of muscle coordination.

Add 1 drop of tea tree oil to the toothpaste on the toothbrush, or add 2 drops of tea tree essential oil to 1 cup of mouthwash. Use the wwproducts as you normally would. Rinse your mouth with water and spit out—*do not swallow.*

OH HONEY

Try to find raw, organic, natural honey without added chemicals that can irritate the skin. You can also add a small amount of baking soda, such as ½ teaspoon, to the Complexion Clearer above for an additional antibacterial boost to fight blemishes, though the baking soda will add grittiness.

ATHLETE'S FOOT FIGHTER

1 drop tea tree essential oil

1 drop oregano essential oil

12 drops carrier oil such as olive, coconut, jojoba, or almond oil

Mix the oils in a small bowl. Apply to the affected area. Wash your hands thoroughly, and avoid touching your eyes or mouth.

Additional Recipes

While the following clean self-care recipes do not use any of the key ingredients listed earlier in this chapter, they definitely come in handy.

NATURAL ORAL CARE

Dilute hydrogen peroxide 1:1 with water and gargle with it for one minute to use as an antiseptic mouthwash. DO NOT swallow this mixture. The hydrogen peroxide in the mouthwash will also whiten teeth gradually. Additionally, the mixture is an effective disinfectant for toothbrushes, retainers, and mouthguards.

CLEAN NATURAL DEODORANT

¼ cup cornstarch

¼ cup baking soda

4–5 tablespoons coconut oil

8–10 drops preferred essential oil (florals and woods are particularly nice)

Combine the cornstarch and baking soda in a small saucepan over low heat. Add the coconut oil 1 tablespoon at a time, gently stirring, until the consistency is like bread dough. Remove the pan from the heat and add the essential oil, stirring continuously. Spoon the mixture into a small glass or silicone bowl and allow to cool. Store covered.

Apply a light coating to underarms using your fingers (best) or a spoon. Baking soda can be abrasive to some, so substitute arrowroot powder or adjust your baking soda amounts if needed.

The mix will remain hard at temperatures below 75°F, so before applying you might need to remove the lid and briefly heat the container for a few seconds in the microwave or in a pan of warm water to soften the contents.

A WORD OF WARNING

Never apply full-strength hydrogen peroxide to mucous membranes (mouth, nose, lips) and *never* swallow it.

Actions You Can Take

SEED

Read your labels. This may not sound like a green tip at all, but a lot of our practices are on automatic. We pick the same face wash because it is the same brand that our parents used. Through these habits, we keep telling producers that no further innovation is necessary. By reading the labels and becoming aware of the ingredients you're regularly putting on your body, you can start to break the cycle and seek out new, clean, and green self-care products.

SPROUT

Try a few natural personal care recipes. Changing your routine can be daunting (especially if it's been working for you), but these recipes are so easy and your body will thank you for it. Start small with one and slowly gather the necessary ingredients for the recipes that work best for you. The components are usually pretty cheap and, once you try one recipe, less of a cognitive leap for you to try another as well. Test out a few of them and, if any of them give you pause, talk about using them with your primary care physician or dermatologist.

TREE

Try clean eating. With the assistance of a healthcare professional, try a clean eating diet to reduce the amount of toxins in your life. By reducing your consumption of prepackaged foods and fast food, you can remove some harmful toxins in your environment and reduce the demand for them in the world around you. Practice safe, healthy, and conscious consumption.

Closing

If you've read this entire book, we thank you! You've learned a ton of information about different topics in personal health, environmental concerns, and sustainability. It can seem like a daunting task to try to change our personal habits in the face of enormous global problems, but there is a lot of reason for hope! There are 7 billion of us on this little blue marble in space—7 billion souls whose everyday actions mold and rearrange mountains, rivers, and forests across the globe. The energy we expend doing that each day is immeasurable, and yet we keep going.

There is no creature or force on Earth with more destructive—or creative—power than the mass of humanity. The key to making our world the best place it can be is to harness that power. And that process starts with each of us doing our part.

We can't keep acting as if the world is an infinite space with inexhaustible resources. We must consider the long-term consequences of our actions when making choices about how we live. From the places we choose to live to the products we choose to use, making sustainable choices is critical to the future of our species—and all of life on Earth.

One person can make a difference! Just look at Greta Thunberg; she was a preteen girl who was worried about climate change. So, she made a sign and went on strike from school to protest her country's seeming lack of concern about the issue. In 2020, she was nominated for a Nobel Peace Prize. The 2021 nominees included an Israeli environmentalist. (As of this writing, the winner has not been announced.)

You don't have to go to these lengths to have a positive impact on the environment. By taking steps to change how you think and live—and encouraging others to do the same—you can make a difference.

Resources

National Resources Defense Council (NRDC) is a leading nonprofit and environmental advocacy group dedicated to protecting the planet and the people who inhabit it; they provide resources to help inform the public of, and implement, clean energy solutions. **nrdc.org**

Environmental Working Group (EWG) is a nonprofit dedicated to making sure everyone can make the wisest and healthiest choices for themselves and their families. They regularly publish consumer guides on things such as ingredients and toxicity of items like sunscreen and household cleaners. **ewg.org/consumer-guides**

UN Environment Programme (UNEP) is the leading global environmental authority. In addition to providing research and resources, the UNEP's main work is not only setting up goals in sustainable development, but also implementing policies to make it a reality for all. **unep.org**

How2Recycle is a standardized labeling system for any recyclable materials in the United States. In the event that you don't know how to recycle a particular item, you can review its list of codes and their respective meanings. **how2recycle.info/labels**

Earth911 helps people understand how to recycle certain items, but also provides a comprehensive, location-based database on how to recycle anything—even hard-to-recycle items. **earth911.com**

Environmental Defense Fund (EDF) is a top nonprofit advocacy group dedicated to providing environmental solutions using economic policies, law, and education. **edf.org**

The **Yale Center for Environmental Law & Policy** is a joint venture between the Yale School of the Environment and Yale Law School that does leading research into climate and sustainability. **envirocenter.yale.edu**

Plastic-Free July is one of the largest groups in the zero-waste movement; while it encourages people to ditch plastic for a single month, it provides tips and tricks that could be used all year round. **plasticfreejuly.org**

Greenpeace is one of the most highly visible and prominent environmental groups. It affects policy, takes direct actions to help the environment, and works to educate the masses, largely through consumer research reports. **greenpeace.org/usa**

Metric Equivalents

Please note that all conversions are approximate.

LIQUID CONVERSIONS

US	Metric
1 tsp	5 ml
1 tbs	15 ml
2 tbs	30 ml
3 tbs	45 ml
¼ cup	60 ml
⅓ cup	75 ml
⅓ cup + 1 tbs	90 ml
⅓ cup + 2 tbs	100 ml
½ cup	120 ml
⅔ cup	150 ml
¾ cup	180 ml
¾ cup + 2 tbs	200 ml
1 cup	240 ml
1 cup + 2 tbs	275 ml
1¼ cups	300 ml
1⅓ cups	325 ml
1½ cups	350 ml
1⅔ cups	375 ml
1¾ cups	400 ml
1¾ cups + 2 tbs	450 ml
2 cups (1 pint)	475 ml
2½ cups	600 ml
3 cups	720 ml
4 cups (1 quart)	945 ml
1 gallon	3.8 L (1,000 ml is 1 liter)

WEIGHT CONVERSIONS

US/UK	Metric
½ oz	14 g
1 oz	28 g
1½ oz	43 g
2 oz	57 g
2½ oz	71 g
3 oz	85 g
3½ oz	100 g
4 oz	113 g
5 oz	142 g
6 oz	170 g
7 oz	200 g
8 oz	227 g
9 oz	255 g
10 oz	284 g
11 oz	312 g
12 oz	340 g
13 oz	368 g
14 oz	400 g
15 oz	425 g
1 lb	454 g

Index

Image Credits